To Shoot Hard Labour 2

To Shoot Hard Labour 2

The Life and Times of Samuel Smith
An Antiguan Working Man
1877–1982

Sir Keithlyn Smith

Indo American Books
2261, Ground Floor, Hudson Line,
Kingsway Camp, Delhi-110 009 (INDIA)
E-mail: sales@iabooks.com, www.iabooks.com

1. Smith Samuel, 1877-1982
2. Antigua – History
3. Social Condition
4. Smith, Samuel, 1877,1982 i11. Title

Title:
To Shoot Hard Labour 2: The Life and Times of Samuel "Papa Sammy" Smith
An Antiguan Working Man.

Author
Sir Keithlyn Smith

Cover painting and pencil illustration of Lady Jumbia: Karim Smith
Map illustration: Karim Smith
Book layout, cover and text design: Lynrod Douglas

Book Team
President : Vijay Sharma
Sr. Vice President : Puneet Singh (London)
Vice President : Kanika Sharma (London)
Pre-Press : P. K. Mishra
Vice-President Marketing : Agnel Henry
Editorial : Sunil Dutt

ISBN: 93-82661-28-X

Published and Digitally Printed in India in 2015
with permission from the copyright holder by:
Indo American Books (IA Books)
2261, Ground Floor, Hudson Line, Kingsway Camp
Delhi 110009, INDIA. Ph.: 91-011-42870094
Email: sales@iabooks.com
Web: www.iabooks.com

To My Family

To My Family

Acknowledgements

The publication of the first edition of To Shoot Hard Labour aroused great interest in the work of the second. I have been energized by many educators, historians and business persons and I am thankful. Among them are Clarvis Joseph, Freddie Jarvis, Austin Josiah, Tim Hector, Selvin Walter, Norris Scholar, Robert Barrett, Elderfield Smith, Dr. Anthony Richards, Ernie Letby,

Sen. Aziz Hadeed, Britton Foreman, Collie Gardner, Elaine Edwards, Hans Burtkupin, West Indies Oil Company (WIOC), British West Indian Airways (BWIA), Sandals Resort, Mark Macfee of Cable & Wireless WI Ltd, Antigua Commercial Bank, Bank of Nova Scotia and Oscar Fredericks.

Thanks to Lila Simon, Dawn (Brooks) Meade, Leone Carr, Brenda Ashe, Helen Looby, Monique Roberts, David Massiah, Avery Jonas, Arif Jonas, Anderson Carty, Leila Jonas, Nella Smith, Holmes Smith, Philmore John, Lynette Nicholas, Gavin Smith, Dawn O'Reggio, Dian O'Reggio and Neya Charles for their unselfish assistance on the manuscript.

I am deeply touched by the advice of the editor Glentis Goodwin and his wife Enid. The enthusiasm of his assistants, Tulsa Beazer, Althea Sharon Smith, Geraldine Emmanuel and Liza Beazer. Their insights and sensitivity did much to enhance the quality of the work.

I attach great value to Agnes Watson Meeker for the photographs pertaining to the Antigua Sugar Factory and her interest in the project. To Aunt Drucilla Smith Richards for providing the cover photo. To Karim

Smith for the sketch map of the Pleasure Ride and other works of art in the project. To my wife Lady Evelyn for designing the cover and to Joseph Jones and Thaddeus Pryce for taking the pictures. Sincere thanks to Adeline Fleming for providing the ancient English coins.

I remember with love and affection my beloved father Hilson Smith for his advice and input. Thanks to Jarelyn Smith, John Smith, Lloyd Smith and Nadine Smith for helping with the proofreading and the general organization of the work.

I am particularly grateful to Jeannette Smith Henderson. Her interest is reflected in the foreword.

Out of the first edition came many outstanding students, Patrick Naylor of England can best be described as having the distinction to be among the honour students who graduated summa cum laude and valedictorian from the University of Papa Sammy.

I feel heavily indebted to the many people known and unknown who found pleasure in associating and promoting the legacy of Samuel "Papa Sammy" Smith. I am profoundly thankful.

Table of Contents

Acknowledgements 7

Foreword 11

Introduction 13

1   WIDENING THE PATH: 17
Undeniable glory of the early people...

2   MORE MONEY LESS WORRY: 35
Pressure on all sides...

3   MOTHER, LEADER, TEACHER, DAREDEVIL: 41
Memory of the last slave from Yag

4   TACKLING THE PROBLEM: 48
Determined to live a better life...

5   PUTTING UP VILLAGES: 64
Hard work, fun and love to the proper

6   TOTAL CALAMITY: 78
The grandeur of Hawksbill faded

7   THE NEW GOLDEN TEXT: 94
Moravian and Methodist condemned

8   CULTURE BLOOMS: 105
People yearn for school

9   SUSTAINING LIFE: 127
Wonder of countless ages

10   SCORCHED EARTH: 142
An orgy of crimes and destruction

11   THE GREAT CONTRAST: 153
Depending on massa and not themselves

12   CHANGING TIMES: 165
Local teachers took charge

13   POWERFUL FORCES AT WORK: 179
Judicial power and obeah culture

14   PAPA SAMMY, THE METEOLOGIST: 197
Points the way forward

15   A BRIEF WEATHER HISTORY....................209-212

Foreword

When Antigua and Barbuda was preparing to celebrate its independence from Britain in 1981, my father Keithlyn Smith took Papa Sammy to see how the city was being decorated and I accom-panied them. After seeing the city Papa Sammy suggested that we should visit some spots where ex-slaves had put up villages. The trip took several hours and encompassed the northern, southern and western parts of the island of Antigua.

Prior to that time, I had no idea that the ex-slaves had at one time established their own villages around the island. I was amazed when Papa Sammy kept telling my father the names by which the different villages were called. I learned from their conversation that my father had been with him on similar trips several times and my great grandfather emphasized again and again that he must not keep the knowledge to himself.

Since that day, I began to awaken to the deficiency in the education that I had been receiving. I am thankful to be included on similar trips between 1981 and 82. In hindsight, I now believe that Papa Sammy had some presentiment of his impending death, and recognized the trip of September 1982 as his last. I realized that the "history" imparted to young and old minds alike, was fashioned to perpetuate the image of how the British Empire flexed its power against the rest of the world by waging numerous wars. I became disturbed when I found out that history books written by descen-dents of ex-slaves also boasted on how Britain's Nelson,

Hawkins, Drake, and others outwitted their European rivals, the might of the British empire, of the deeds of kings and presidents of colonial pow-ers but mentioned nothing about the forces that shaped our own his-tory. During my tenure as a student at the Antigua Girls' High School, nothing was taught about what happened to our ancestors, and to this day, the silence is telling indeed. Despite the wave of nationalism that was begun by the British Caribbean people in the late 1930's and their subsequent independence from their colonial masters, Caribbean leaders have entrusted British scholars to write our history. It is not wise for them to think that our colonial masters would confess to the horrors they perpetuated on our forefathers through the vehicles of slavery and colonization. They failed to see that there had been a conspiracy all through the years to keep the truth from our people. In fact, their quest was to completely erase our past. Such pursuit I believe is being thwarted by the first publi-cation of "To Shoot Hard Labour", which made a tremendous impact on people of all races and pointed a new direction for our Caribbean historians. Both volumes are competing for first place in my heart, but I will leave it up to the readers to judge which volume is preferred.

Papa Sammy urgently calls for us to begin to search meaningfully for our identity and our true history. During the years in the universities in North America and the Caribbean, I found many institutions of learning to be promoting the rich history told in To Shoot Hard Labour. The new To Shoot Hard Labour 2 provides more detail of the lives of black people in the Caribbean and the western world as a whole.

This new text also brings a broader understanding of the day to day life of our people as they strive to overcome slavery, colo-nialism and other contemporary issues. I feel honored to be part of this great project that will forever be a source of joy to the family and an inspiration to millions around the world.

Jeanette Smith Henderson, LLB. J.D. B.A.

Introduction

To Shoot Hard Labour 2 is a continuation of the original book To Shoot Hard Labour which tells of the life and times of Samuel "Papa Sammy" Smith, an Antigua working man who lived from 1877 – 1982.

Part 2 tells how the ex-slaves defended with pride, their symbol of freedom and of how succeeding generations did not... How the planters finally succeeded in erasing, almost without a trace, the symbol of the free people. How they were forced back to the plantation. It tells of the kind of society that developed, and the excruciating misery in which they lived and died for nearly a century afterwards.

According to Papa Sammy, the planters played for time while the inexperienced off-springs of ex-slaves were growing increasingly indifferent to the avowed aim of the planters to subject them to slave conditions. The Antiguan masters used the Jamaican riot of 1865 as a pretext to abolish the General Assembly and returned the island to Crown Colony rule. In doing so, they sought to create the ideal stage to pursue and eventually achieve their manifest destiny – kill king and rule country – accountable to no one. Groans could not be heard at "master control" four thousand miles away.

Slavery was abolished in Antigua and Barbuda in 1834. While Europe's push for technology may be one of the main causes for abolition, the United States (U.S.A) expansion of cotton, sugar and tobacco in the mid nineteenth century increased the demand for slave labour. Cuba imported slaves up to 1865 and Brazil carried on the trade for a while longer. Thus the uncertainty created in the planters' world after 1834, gave rise to the emergence of pro-slavery sentiment once again. The freed slaves were leaving plantation life to establish free villages – the symbol of a free people. The Antiguan planters were forced to import Portuguese labour to perform tasks left undone by the freed slaves. The Chief of Police led the call for the re-introduction of slavery. Between 1834 and 1866, the Antiguan planters took every conceivable action to halt the setting up of free villages. According to Papa Sammy, there were 68 – 70 of them. Planters vowed that the symbol of the free people must be destroyed. After all, the English were a people self-ordained to rule the world – the greatest people God's omnipotence had created. The glory and the happiness and the security of the two British subjects must be restored. The freedom flame must be extinguished and the down trodden people made to genuflect unquestionably to the echo of "Rule Britannia". Within that period, the freed slaves were developing a culture that distanced itself from any tinge of that which slave masters enforced on them over the centuries of slavery. Vilified and victimized, the ex-slaves were considered to be nothing more than the wretched of the earth. Daring to leave the plantation, living independently in huts and further refused to work. They were led by women determined to fight rather than return under the control of the masters. These women leaders were experienced, fearsome, fearless and created an impregnable path.

The enormity of the price paid on life, blood and property by the blacks is found in the powerful testimony of Lady Jumbia, the Goodwin family and Papa Sammy's mother, to name a few. Part 2 also tells how the Portuguese were treated differently to the blacks and how the English planters attempted to restrict the advancement of the Portuguese in trade and commerce; and how both the English and Portuguese prevented blacks from engaging in similar businesses. It was anathema for a planter to propose marriage to a black woman. The inevitable consequence was a courtship with death. The policy of any governor that was geared towards the improvement of the lives of the blacks, was scornfully pushed aside or reluctantly carried out.

To Shoot Hard Labour 2 gives account of an important journey of the Goodwin family during which they retraced the foot path of the Aborigines. It dispels the notion that the colonial masters surveyed the land from scratch. Those foot paths, in fact, formed the basis for the original groundwork for the road construction in Antigua and Barbuda. It tells of the efforts of Governor Haynes Smith to improve the health and education services, the law courts and the gradual closing of estate prisons as the 20th century progressed. It tells of the slow but steady replacement of the English midwives, teachers and other workers in the Civil Service and the attitude of the blacks that replaced them.

Papa Sammy could not hide the displeasure he felt against some of the top Antiguan scholars of the 20th century. He accused them of deliberately taking the truth out of our history. "They kept on writing and talking the planter's way". He would so often accuse them of being ashamed of their past and he would say over and over again, "If the Lord help all you to write, don't attempt to please any body, just write wa me say – na water dung nuttem me say".

Dr. Eric Williams, Prime Minister of Trinidad and Tobago (1961-1981) said in his book from *Columbus to Castro*, "*all we can boast about is a few monographs, the product of Metropolitan Scholarship that has been fragmented, irregular, sporadic and often pathetically inaccurate and prejudice. Few colonials have to date extended their nationalism to the cultural field and dedicated themselves to the task of writing or rewriting where necessary, their own history*".

Papa Sammy's account of our history is a microscopic part of the stories told by tens of thousands who preceded him – those in his time and those who followed. He spoke with insight of the fact that storytelling would cease to be an important part of everyday life. And so in the 1960's, he became what we would call a drill master and operated like a man having a race against time with all he was trying to tell.

The many times we journeyed through the pleasure ride to various places where the slaves established villages, the repeated long periods we spent at the Hawksbill area and many more places of interest in the land, he would urge that we learn and inwardly digest his teachings. He would repeat some more of his famous words "you must know your own land", because as he would put it, "bright people would say otherwise". He was also fond of saying, "Me mouth nah Bible. Check it out if you can, what you hear from me. What is certain is that I give it exactly as I know it and I expect you to do the same".

Well respected, not so much for his age but for his immense knowledge, his humility, persistence and consistency in which he would hand down his stories, he was also admired, not only by his village people, but by those with whom he worked and associated, and in particular, by the generation that knew him during his final twenty years.

It is impossible to commit to print the abundance of information that flowed from his lips. To Shoot Hard Labour and To Shoot Hard Labour 2 are merely a truncated version of his life and times.

King Ras Frank-I wrote in his critical review of the first publication; "Your grandfather is no longer solely yours, you have given him to us".

And so said all of us!

1

WIDENING THE PATH:

Undeniable glory of the early people

I have no doubt that the early people[1] could get around this land. I also believe that most of them would live in areas that have water and where they could grow food. How these people move around was a thing I learn as I grow older.

The Goodwin family[2] always say that it would not be correct for anyone to say that the English start to survey and build roads from scratch because they did meet foot paths throughout the land. And the English follow most of the foot paths when they make the main roads in the early days. The footpaths he said was just narrow. That would suggest that the people then, walk behind one another. The English find heavy stones space in the centre of the foot paths. The average distance that was between each stone was about 20 yards. The belief was that the stones make it easy for them to keep on track and find where they want to go. The large stones

---

[1]Carib, Arawaks, and Ciboney, the indegenous people that lived in Antigua before the Europeans took charge. People also refer to them as the beforetime people.

[2]A prominent and influental plantocrat family that lived in Antigua.

put in the foot path could also be a guide when rain come and grass spring up and cover the track. The beforetime people, me think, would also use them as a means of communication to others who may travel on the road for the first time. One of my old boss, George Goodwin explain that there were two heavy stones where foot roads cross and three would be at the foot of the hills. That, he think, would point out the way to the hill top where some of them live.

If I may say this, the beforetime people do not have to be only what the English people call Caribs or Arawaks or the latest one I here a lot about in my old days, the Cibonies. Other people could come from anywhere and own the land long garling time[3]. People we would not even dream about. Before I get to know so many things from the Goodwins, I never know, or put it rightfully, it never dawn on me or a tell you, it never even come up in me mind that other people use to live on the land before Columbus reach here.

The main place of business for the beforetime people, was along the sea shore and on the hill tops. From what use to be around on top of Green Castle Hill, it strikes me as if up there was the show-piece for them people. A chair made out of stone and a stone bowl, along with plenty different stone carving and other things was there. There was the large water bowl carve out of stone at the bottom. This generation make Mericans[4] mash um up. The bowl was a sure sign that some kind of ceremony use to take place there. Another bowl that was similar to that, was at Morris Plantation right at the foot of the hill and that also garn[5]. The round south hotel build right where it was. The people that are now in front, pass cure. They allow Mericans to be blowing down Green Castle Hill to make house blocks. Say after me, it won't be long before them blow priceless Green Castle flat. Shame! This man here, always have plenty pain when me see treasure that man can't

3. Very long time ago.

4. Americans

5. No longer existed.

buy nor mek, blow up intc
have the same stone and n
leaders could not do better

There was the evide
people could do plenty clin
problems following the path
them. Some of the foot path
English widen the path or cι
ones they meet.

In 1899, some of R.S ....ny and friends with
whom I work, set off to walk in the path that they think the beforetime people used to tread. A whole gang a them. They determine
that it was a thing that they must accomplish before the century
move on. It was a custom for some planters to retread what they
call Arawak footprints at certain times. I was not working with the
Goodwins for much time and I did not think they would want me
to follow them. Then again, I would not want to be with them. I
think that they were too happy. In the end, I have no choice. Off
with them I had to go. They walked with plenty food. I remember
that they take the north side one Saturday and continue till they
completed it some Saturdays after. Then after that they travel the
south side. They walk every Saturday until they think they complete
the old tracks that the beforetime people use to travel.

The journey turn out to be a good, good exercise for me. It
was much more refreshing than I ever think it could be. They could
not cover all the ways, but the young people then get a good piece
of knowledge of what they always hear bout. And it was long after
that joy walk, that I realize the amount of knowledge I got from that
journey. There was hardly any place that I travel after that did not
take in part of the area that the group cover during that memorable
end of the century walk. I can't forget how R.S.D. Goodwin would
take out the map from time to time and point out the name of the
particular spot to his people.

There were two main winding foot roads that show that

around the island. One start from north of Rat
ner from south of Rat island. Rat island is a little
he shape like a rat. It is attach to the west end of the
e to what is known as Fort James. So one would under-
hy people call the little lump of earth, Rat Island.

The beforetime people foot Road North of Rat Island, run
rom where people use to call Cove and Forth Bay, and pass through
Ledwell and through Runaway Bay and Dickenson Bay through
Soldier Point and Boons Point into Boons Chair. That foot road also
take the edge of the whole north coast through Beggers Point and
come all the way around Winthropes Bay and Barnacle Point and
travel all the way around until it hit on Byam Bay and run onto
Parham, then into Crabbs and further on to the northeast end at the
tip of North Sound Point. There was also the track from Parham
Bay that go right across the upper middle of the island, from north
to south and stretch all the way east of the All Saints Church. That
track, hits right on Monks Hill.

The foot path that travel south of Rat Island, also was of the
same winding pattern. This foot road take the edge of what is now
the city seashore and go south into Greenbay and move southwest
to the shore line of Yepton and Galley Bay, and wind all through to
Jolly Beach, then to Fryes and Hyde Estates through Urlings and
Brooks and Cades Peak, and Ruins and Sage Hill, then unto Follies
and wind all around through Swetes, then through Mount Williams
and join up with Monks Hill. There was the Monks Hill foot path
that meet with the one coming from the extreme north of the island
which continues and hit on the southeast sea front. Another important foot path was the one that use to run from Gray Hill through
Cooks Hill and right on the circular Range Hill. That foot road
leads unto Green Castle Hill and to the other range of hills in the
mid south, and run to Haliday Hill to Sageness right onto the main
south track. That foot track also leads right into Fig Tree Hill and
Uooge Hill.

The English also meet two foot paths that they use to refer

to as the two main foot paths that run east to west of the land. They run from extreme west to extreme east. One was from Mount Thomas area, near Hawksbill seaside, in the west, and travel right through Cooks Estate, through Ottos into Herberts and wind its way through to Indian Town, and hit on the foot of Fancy Cove. The other one connect Reeds Point in the southwest; that include a path of the Jolly Beach area and then travel in a curve and twist through the east and all the way to Rickets Bay; and they would get to Green Island how they can. Green Island was one of the chief place to find the beforetime people on that side. Foot paths would have branch off tracks that would lead to many hill tops. There were tracks on all sides of Green Castle Hill. Two of them lead to Ebenezer, and another to Dunnings; and these two lead to the main south track.

Just at the turn of the eighteenth century, slavery in Antigua began to pick up steam. The English Massas started to trunk up the land between them like them wild. As you look round they devour up the deep south, central south and southwest. I get the story that there was one particular Bakkra that the people use to say was more greedy than all the rest. He was one Massa Ruin. They use to call him Greedy Ruin. At one time according to the Goodwins he pawn up almost all the land in the deep south, central south and the southwest. That was the area where water was easy to get and the growing of food was easier on that side.

The early Massas had to fix up them foot paths. They widen them and straighten them out as far as possible. This was to accomodate the horse and cart and the buggy which at the time use to pull Massa sugarcane, carry the food and take him around. R.S.D. Goodwin say that the Codrington family was the first to bring a horse and cart to Antigua in the 1670's. That was confined mostly to his estate, because the roads were not there. To cut roads in most of the land was not that hard, says R.S.D. Goodwin because the English follow a good number of tracks of the beforetime people. Naturally, they would build more roads and would have more barricades, because of the way they mark out the different cane fields and estates. The Goodwin's famous comment was "one thing for sure, whoever the beforetime people were, they surely were no fools. They did know the land very well".

The cutting of the road in the south, he explain, was the most trying to work on. In many instances, there was no other way to lay out the road differently to how the English meet them. To widen some areas, in order to get away from the cliffs, take some life. The early planters could not imagine how the beforetime people walk on some of the edges. It take a lot of risks to cut some of the roads away form the cliff. I would be glad to know the name, people call the south foot path. The English named it the Bermudan Valley. No one told me the reason for the name. But long time now the slaves drop off Bermudan, and up to now everybody just say "the Valley".

There was quite a few parts of the Valley foot road that cause a lot of problem to widen. One was the path near Darkwood and running southward round the corner. There is where people used to call Crabb Point. The people use to say that a big shark was always lurking around the shore to devour anyone that fall off the edge. This is a dangerous spot up to right now.

If a vehicle slip now, it would surely slide into the sea. That was the same thing and worse with the horse and cart then. Another one is the part when travelling over the hill from Morris Plantation to where we now call Curtain Bluff at the west end of Old Road. We use to call that place The Bad Sea. Lately, they put up a wall and they now call it The Bad Sea Wall. I think though, that the part that give the most trouble to widen, was the area that start from the southwestern end of a piece of land that use to belong to Greedy Ruin and continue through Tremontain and through another piece of land that was for Greedy Ruin again and pass through Signal hill and Sage Hill and end up on land for Massa Wallings.

For sure, the English did not deviate much from the beforetime people foot road. They just follow the shape of the hills. That cause a deeper bend in the road. The road on top the hill end up like the letter U. The bakkra call the hill like the letter U itself. The U Hill they use to call it. But the slaves would rename it Uooge Hill. The word give them trouble to call and later the bakkra that owned the hill was known by the slaves as Massa Uooge. The drop from the cliff was deep. Plenty deeper than what it is now. When anybody slip into the deep, at that point, just say them gone a guassa. At the time of the widening of the road, many slaves fall to their deaths.

The bakkra come up with the plan to tie them with rope around the waist and then tie them on nearby trees. When they slip, the rope would save them from the death drop, but they would still get damage. The jerk would still hurt the body.

The available tool the people had to work with, at the time, was picks, matocks and sledge. A fork and a shovel would become handy now and again. But you would imagine the kind of labour they must shoot to get through the hard stone and rock. At first, the Massas cut the road to allow a single horse and cart to pass at a time. That did not provide enough width to prevent the carriage from sliding into the deep easily.

For several years, all the traffic around the valley was down hill. The hill was too rugged, steep and risky for animals to pull the cart over. The people today would have to use their imagination and think on what the situation was then. That spot is a far cry today, from what it was. The chances of sliding backwards when going up hill and eventually drop into the deep was too great a risk. A big risk a-tell-you, don't mind all they do. But the travel dung hill had problems too. The groom had to guide the animal dung the hill. That is, walking with it and holding the rein close to the bit in order to control the speed. If one person was on the cart, that person would come off and guide the animal down the hill the same way. The young people back then would say, the journey was not sweet if they have to walk down. The ride down was the thing! At times, the animal would stumble and force to start to trot or quicken the pace. Look out! Away inna the deep, the carriage may end up. Although down hill ride was the thing, the bulk of the bakkra would always come off and walk and allow the groom to guide the carriage down and slaves would provide brakes from behind.

In 1709 or there about, the Planters come up with a plan to plant wild fig[6] at the edge of the cliff. That would be from the bottom of Tremontain Hill to the top of Uooge Hill. The idea was that the wild fig would catch root quick and would form a blind and a barricade. The thinking then was that the barricade would stop the carriage in the event of a slide.

Not seeing below, would also take the fear out of man and animal. The bakkra call the spot between Tremontain Hill and Uooge Hill, Fig Tree Hill. Before I get the story of Fig Tree Hill, I use to believe that man coun't walk for fig on the Hill, and who ever pass that way would get plenty fig to eat and carry home. After I get to know, I realize why I never see a bunch of fig growing there. The wild fig did not take hold as the bakkra think it would. Some did ketch root, but could not find the soil to get the firmness and so form the strong barricade intended.

As time roll by, more and more planters pour into the land and the Valley Road get fast. Some would ignore the danger and take the chances. The happy ones, mostly the young, and particularly, them that just get a new sweetheart or just married, would travel round the island on the buggy and down Fig Tree Hill would not pass them. Please don't tell them not to walk down. That was not sweet. Down hill they would ride just for the sport.

A big story for the planters was that during the Christmas season of 1714, the carriage of the newly married, Clive Dupont and his wife, get way into the gully. The fig tree fence did not mean a thing. That could not stop the carriage and the new bride and groom from droping over. They did not come out alive. Their friends that was following behind their carriage, also drop over and Fig Tree Hill claim the lives of six people one time.

---

6. A tree with some strong roots that grow very tall. It does not bear fig the local term
   people use for banana.

The Goodwins say that for a long time, the Planters were mortally afraid to travel on that side. The people fraid both the danger of the hill and the Dupont family Jumbies. People use to claim that the jumbies moless almost everybody that pass along the way. Most people would try them level best not to be on that road after the sun sink below the trees.

Some of the bakkra use to make a lot of joke over the Dupont jumbies. One of the joke was, anybody that pass in the area was sure to dream of the Dupont bride and groom. They would bound to see the Dupont in their sleep and the husband pulling the ring off the wife finger.

After the Fig Tree Hill accident, one Governor Matthew that was in charge at the time, decide that don't mine how long the road take to widen properly it must be done. Wah me hear, was that the Governor say that even if it take a whole year to chip away one stone, the road must be made wide enough to prevent belly gripe like that of the Dupont. The bakkra realize that the wild fig trees did not grow into the strong fence but give the false assurance that they could prevent things from toppling over the cliff. The massas pluck out everyone of the wild fig tree.

Some young people was deadly harden like the Dupont family. Young people, in any age, think hard fu tek heed.[7] They would hear, again and again, that they must unlight, and someone must guide the animal down the hill while the slaves provide the brakes. Quite a number of them would be so full of glee, that they did not think for a moment that glee can turn sour in the twinkling of an eye.

Govenor Matthew left before the work actually get to start. The next governor, one Hamilton, cousin to the Dupont, begin to widen the hill. The work was slow and cumbersome. Sickness and death to the slaves slow down the work and it eventually come to a stop for about five years in a row.

The Planters restart the work in 1724, and by the end of

7. Refuse to comply with order or rules.

1725, it look as if it would never done. In that year, more people dead-out than quite a few years put together. The angel of death was so rampant that only one single slave, from a gang of more than fifty, that was working at the Fig Tree Hill road, escape death. Well, to me, only them that born with silver spoon in them mouth, get way from death that year. The big rumor around the place was that the Dupont jumbies was the angel of death, and was killing all them that work on the hill. That was just a big joke. Death was not only for them that work on the Fig Tree Hill neck, but it was throughout the whole island. Every corner of the land get some touch off.

The Planters use to remember 1725 as the year of sorrow. I remember the Goodwins to say, the slave population in that year was about 25,000 and that a quarter of it pass off within the first ten months of that year. I think I am seeing his face when he use to say, 'they nearly did not have place to bury people'.

I remember asking him what kill them, if they were put to shoot too much hard labour and starve on top of that? But he usually smile and say, 'Sammy, fever kill most of them'.

After some real hard labour, Fig Tree Hill and Uooge Hill road become much safer. That was some time towards the end of the 1720's. There was a little more room away from the edge. They fit in the flint stone as tight as they could get them. The road was still rugged and steep, but the carriage could then travel down hill as well as up hill with some assurance that they won't fall that easily into the deep. That was the relief No stopping on the path. The massas call the road the Pleasure Ride!

Them min out of them kin[8]. Don't ask if them bakkra was happy. They decide that this pleasure ride must start at the Mother Country Church in Falmouth under Monks Hill and end up on Running Bridge Hill near Green Castle. That was the stop for the picnic. Picnic in those days, was not at the seaside as people do today. It was on top of hills or in the caps.[9] Most of the massas always want a non-stop pleasure ride mostly when they take the

8. Very excited.
9. In a wooded area.

spree for the first time. In those days lots of churches were on the way. The Mother Country had a church for every two miles of the pleasure ride. The road touch on all the Mother Country Church around the Valley. The pleasure ride hold the best scenery of the land. The long line of trees high on both sides of the road, hide the sun. The twist and turns along with the high trees, provide shade almost from the start to the end of the journey. This happen even when the sun was well overhead. Back then, there was not a single dwelling house on the west side of the pleasure ride. Trees of all descriptions lined the route on both sides - It was like a natural umbrella. The branches of some trees would tangle overhead with each other for a long distance.

I am not all sure of the number of springs on the way. I don't know if anyone ever stop to count them. There was the flow from Pussy Spring and Mommy Spring that cross in Liberta. The Planters call the cross the Slaugh. Horse and cart may stick, if care was not taken. The spring that show how nature is really wonderful, is the Tom More Spring. It use to run like a river for just over a mile and it cross the road from south to north four times for the distance. After it flow for about a quarter mile, it cross over from south to north. That cross the people use to call Bridge-A-Peace. And close to the Bridge-A-Peace was the narrowest of the path, two rocks hard to break. Cart could hardly pass through. They call that spot Anvil Eye.

The water flows on the north for about the same distance before it cross back to the south side again. This is the cross people call Ruin Table. A little way down, it cross again back from south to north. This cross people call Ruin Foot Bridge. After it flow for another quarter mile or so, it change back and finally flow at Claremont Gate Bridge and runs through Claremont Estate to the sea. The old time people use to call the spring the River Bed. Most people would wash them foot and hands or drink at the different crosses.

On the journey, there was also the three bridges that carry

the names Faith, Hope and Charity. The most easterly one is Faith, and the other names follow in order. The Warner Spring now call Brookes Spring, was a little way from Charity Bridge. The planters call the spring after Thomas Warner, the man that officially claim the land for the Mother Country. The early planters use to go on as if they must worship Warner at that Spring. They would salute and shout up the name Sir Thomas when they reach there. And there is the Nelson Rock. The planters say Admiral Lord Nelson fired at the rock when he was sailing around Antigua.

On the pleasure ride there was another flow of water that many people use to love to look at. This flow of water people refer to as Bubble Bed . It come from the many springs that run almost in a straight line through Christian Valley and Blover Valley. People used to watch the water, because the water would bubble out of the earth at various places. Most of the water found its way to Yorks Estate then to the sea. The planters use to guide a good portion of it up onto the land of Massa Jennings.

Back then, few planters would take the pleasure ride for the first time and don't go inside Nancy Rock. The old time planters adore Nancy Rock. That was another big point on the journey. The Goodwins used to keep on saying that their old parents take the pleasure ride when the English people celebrate two hundred years of Warner foot prints in the land. They re-walk and kneel at Nancy Rock and some of the other places. Make no mistake, they take the ride in 1899 to close the century. At that time, young and old bakkra make the mark.

The Pleasure Ride is a far cry from what it was then. One of the big difference is the loss of trees on both sides of the path. The running water, that flow along the path of the ride is no longer there. And, all in all, the exiting Pleasure Ride dwindle away like those who found it.

After the crop season of 1900, the Goodwin family that I worked with, decided to take the Pleasure Ride before the year end. It was a big-big celebration for them - I now glad that I did get the opportunity then. It was from that time, I get to understand what was the Pleasure ride that the bakkra talk so much about. Who ever travel that journey would not easily forget the pleasure, the kind of excitement and the feeling that go with it. The Goodwins believed that any one who go on the pleasure ride really enjoyed the undeniable work and glory of the early people. That is the gospel truth.

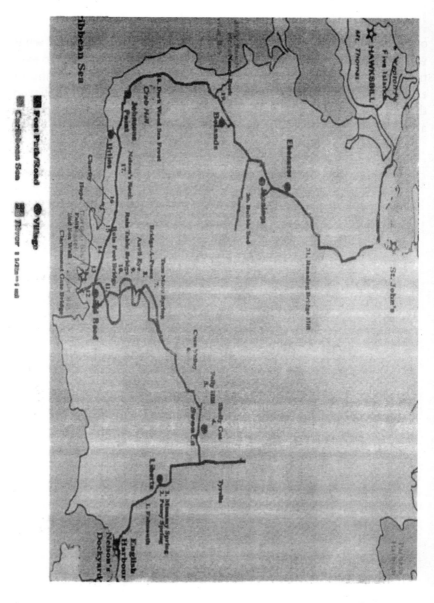

Map shows the physical paths of the pleasure ride, springs and rivers, some of the early foothpaths and villages

Papa Sammy on his one hundreth birthday, January 1, 1977 with Sir Wilfred Jacobs, Govenor General of Antigua and Barbuda.

Cover photo of Papa Sammy at 104 years old, bonding with his great, great, great, grand daughter, Taj.

Ficus of bearded fig tree locally called wild fig or simply, fig tree. This particular type of tree belongs to the "Bearded Fig Tree" family. The term bearded refers to the special roots which hang from the branches in abundance (adventious roots). This tree was planted around the 1720's as a protective barrier against falling over the cliffs at the place we call Fig Tree Hill.

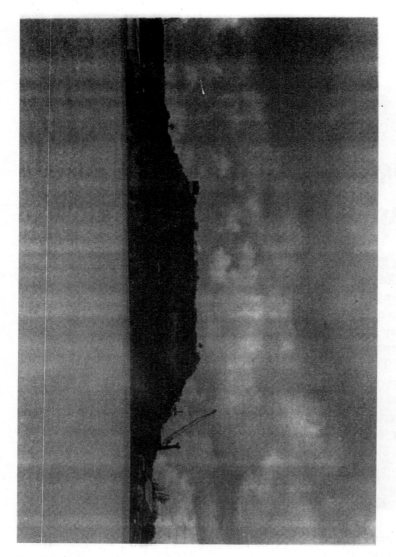

Rat Island in modern times.
Not a separate island, Rat Island is actually a little hill that is shaped like
a rat. It is attatched to the west coast of the island close to the area
known as Forth James. Rat Island was also known as the lepper colony
since it was home to people who suffered from leporsy.

2
MORE MONEY LESS WORRY:
Pressure on all sides

I was lucky to find out long time that the record the Goodwins of Collins Estate have on the abolition of slavery and other happenings was far different to what the preachers, teachers and other people use to drive in the heads of the ex-slave population at weekday school and at Sunday School and quite lately in some newspapers around, and from other people.

The planters always have the true record but the same planters water them down plenty and twist them when they are ready to give them to the people. The aim was that people will swallow everything as gospel truth and become nothing else but proper bakkra 'say after me'.

Slaves and ex-slaves back then would have very little idea of the contents of letters that pass between Governors and Secretary of State or from Magistrates to Governors or to other planters.

To cut a long story short, slaves and ex-slaves would never know fully what the big people write in letters about them and the affairs of the land. I say fully because I am one of the ex-slaves picknee who happen to know just a little because of the little luck that attend me.

What happen to me would surely happen to some others. To

tell you clearly, I do not believe that teachers of ex-slaves ever put hand on them important letters. A tink though that if they ever put hand on them, they would not easily tell people the real story or the truth.

In those days, I was one of the few who get the privilege to read some letters. Me look into them letters again and again. I use to know some of them by heart. My bosses see me looking into them time and again. Not a thing they say! They never one time rebuke me. Me really think they believe that after I throw them back in the corner, everything stay right there. I happen to read the most at the place where I work for long years. That is at Collins and Duers Estates. I remember reading a very special letter that Governor MaGregor send to the Secretary of State in the Mother Country. The letter was telling the Secretary of State the many happenings in Antigua for the year 1833 August to 1834 December. MaGregor was the Governor in the land at the time of the freedom.

The Antiguan planters were deadly against the abolition of slavery. This letter from the Governor mention that the planters are in mourning for the pending loss of the slave trade and that from all indications, the mourning will be long. There was daily quarrel in the land over the decision of the Mother Country to free the slaves. Most of the bakkra could not take it. They just could not change the decision, so they have to go a long with it. Their first argument on the period of prenticeship was that four years was too short. The letter say the masters them argue that it should be at least half a dozen years.

The letter also talk bout running disgruntlement among the slave population in Antigua for a period between 1829 and 1833. That was because some slaves get the feeling that they should be free already. And the question they keep asking was, why should they be the last behind?

MaGregor's letter also mention that for a long period the slaves at Warner and adjoining estates slow down the work. They become too rebellious. They would not believe that no freedom was given yet to slaves in the other lands. The big question they keep asking was "what could be keeping their freedom back so long, when other slaves done get fu them?"

I also learn from the letter that the Anglican Church people wage a bitter war against any form of prenticeship. That was news to me! I never hear bout that. I then get the feeling that this was one of the very few good things the Anglican massas ever do for slaves. MaGregor in his letter also tell the Secretary of State that the argument of the Anglican priests was of two parts. One was that the bulk of the slaves have been patient and God-fearing all along and delay of direct freedom may stir them to anger. The second was, any prenticeship period would not be less expensive than slavery itself. Added to that, prenticeship would mean part ownership of the slaves. That would be too costly and unmanageable. According to MaGregor, there were 29,000 slaves, most of which were able to work and good enough to suit the masters over a long period. He could not foresee any immediate problem with the hands of labour.

I also get to know that the church people argument against prenticeship pick up strength. The letter state that for the first time in the history of the colony, there was serious bitterness between some priests and the rest of the planters. Some planters make them mind up to leave the land and sail back to the Mother Country if slavery really come to an end. According to the Goodwins, a great portion were confused and did not know what direction to follow. Their argument was that sales and trading of slaves between the islands continue up to weeks before the actual arrivance of the freedom. There were some hard headed slave massas who did not accept the fact that slavery would ever come to an end despite all the talk that was going on. On the other hand some were prepared to do as they like regardless.

Massas Francis Shand and Otto Baijer were bitterly against the waiving of the prenticeship. MaGregor in his letter explained that little over two weeks or so before the important vote on the question in the Assembly both men changed their mind and begin to support the argument of the Clergy. The reason they say was the planters would make plenty more money if they forget bout the prenticeship thing. I remember in the MaGregor report he also explain that both Shand and Baijer made it known to the massas who abuse them for their change of heart that it was not love nor mercy they have for the slaves or any human in the land. It was strictly the profit they look at. The Baijers phrase was "more money less worry".

The main reason for their change of heart was that they spend time working out the money part and found out that it would be dog cheaper to let the slaves go right away. Let dem go now[1]. Another argument they use was that far less labour would be needed to operate the plantations. One would understand that the only thing left for the planters to make sure of, was that the ex-slaves would have to shoot hard labour for their money. MaGregor letter explain again that the change of views of Shand and Baijer did not make their side win out one time in the final vote. It was the vote of the Speaker. The Assembly vote even out. Everything was still. Not a word! All sides look to the Speaker and wonder wa side he go tek[2].

The Speaker, one Dr. Nicholas Nugent loose the tie in favour of the Baijer fraction in the Assembly. The stillness of the place break up into a mixture of loud noise, bad wod, threats and laughter. Them nearly fight in the Assembly. One vote save the slaves of Antigua a further four years in bondage. That is how the slaves in this land get freedom in 1834. As important as this is, I only know it because I happen to read it in the planters house not another place. The way some bright people put the story is that the Antigua massa was nice and out of compassion they did not follow the other islands with the prentiship thing. This was also the argument of the church people.

Some people also say that the slaves were warish and that was the reason why there was no prentiship. I think that my biggest

1. Free the slaves now.

2. Which side the speaker will support.

shock come when a bright man, S.A.E. Hill, founder and Principal of the Hill Secondary School, one of the leading teachers in the land, tell the people of Freeman's Village at a Home and Family Festival in 1953 that the Antiguan slaves were fighters and that's why they did not work the prenticeship like the other islands. They refuse to work it. The principal of the Hill Secondary School could tell that to the others but surely, not to me. I mean no disrespect but one of the leading teachers in this land in 1953 was just a big shot bakkra say-after-me about what happen to me and my slave generation, at that time.

Donald Sheppard, member of the Legislative Council and executive member of The Antigua Trades and Labour Union was chairman of the programme. He tell the people, after Teacher Hill gone, that Hill was wrong, wrong. He, Donald Sheppard swear to all god that he is going to write what he know. He also say that the Union must put its history together now because it is the same way that kind of people will twist what really happen. And so often people twist things and it's a wonder how they can fit right into place like gospel. R.S.D. Goodwin say that people twist how the All Saints Anglican Church get the name. The reason they say for the name is because all the parishes meet some where nearby and all the names of the parishes begin with the word saint- All the Saints meet at the spot. R.S.D. Goodwin whose family have a big hand in building the All Saints Anglican Church say some early settlers came from All Saints in England, live in the area before the church came on the scene and call the area All Saints like how some settlers name places Piccadilly, Thames, Newgate, Constitution Hill and other names of places in the Mother Country. In this case, this man won't accuse anyone of deliberatly twisting because both reasoning don't make a big difference. The Goodwins also say there are many English churches that carry the name All Saints and at the same time have nothing to do with the meeting up of All the Saints in the area.

Otto Baijer, owned Ottos Estate at the head of St. John's city at the time of the prenticeship vote. He use to live where we now call Michael's Mount, a little way from the lighthouse on East Street. People call the place Ottos House. When Maurice Michael build the hotel at the same place in the 1960's, me tell Donald, the whole story again. I ask him to use his influence and let them name the hotel Baijer Castle in memory of that deciding vote. Tell the people what happen. Me tell him again the name would not be to honour the slave massas but to draw attention to what take place at the time. I let him know that it would be more proper than to name a new place Glanville Village as was the case. No new village should name after any slave massa. The punishment at Glanville Estate when they say slaves tief was that they put the right hand in hot water, but our people still call a new village, Glanville Village. Sheppard agree with me that the hotel should carry Baijer Castle.

It was understandable that the slave massas would have problems over the change from slave labour to paying for labour. Not all would quite readily understand how to operate to get the maximum profit all at once. Money, money and more money was the object. The ex-slaves would have more serous problems, after the freedom. They would have many questions on them minds. Lots of doubts, although they want this freedom so badly. They were not permitted to gather before the Freedom. They could not get to exchange ideas among each other even when freedom was close at hand.

Just after slavery end the same Speaker of the House of Assembly mark you, the same man that loose the tie on the prenticeship argument, was the same man that decide the work day for the ex-slaves. The Work day must be from sunrise to sunset with two and a half hours break, and from sunset to sunrise with the same length of break for anyone who happen to work the night hours. That was what the older heads call "Nugent hours" or "Nugent time" or "Nugent Labour".

3
MOTHER, LEADER, TEACHER, DAREDEVIL:
The last slave from Yag

Hardly anybody around know about Africa when I was growing up as a young man. Not too many people was around and sensible at the time of the freedom to let us know or give us an idea of the place. The people of Freeman's Village was lucky - lucky. A woman by the name of Jumbia was one of the very few who was born a slave, take part in the whole change, and was alive and Trang[1] and sensible when I was a teenager at Freeman's Village. When I use the word sensible, I mean that she could relate properly the hapennings of she days.

I still count her as the most knowledgeable woman I came across on the life in slavery days, and on some of what happen afterwards. She tell all of us that her mother bring her into this world on the first Monday in July 1821, and that, because she was born on a Monday her people call her Jumbia. They tell she that her father family was from a place call the Old Goat[2] and that he did

1. Strong.
2. Referring to the Gold Coast in Africa.

41

have a sister they call Jumbia. When she grow old, the people call her Lady Jumbia . She was able to keep the name because slavery done before her master sell she. The bakkra in slavery did not know that they call her so. She was a long, long, woman[3]. I get to know her properly after we move to Freeman's Village in 1888.

She use to chat plenty. Sometimes she chat worse than if them heng she mouth over boiling ockra pot[4]. She never stop the boast that she was the only person alive in the village then, that was around when the freedom come.

Jumbia use to tell us where her generation come from. A massa William Joseph landed at Parham with her generation from Nigeria in 1638. He stop off at Parham, and select a sight call Stony Hill for them to live. I recall that in the early days, the slave massas did not want slave to pack up near them. There was not many slaves then. Running away would hardly be in their minds. The early massas did not expect slaves to runaway. However, to avoid that, the massas control tools, food and clothes.

Jumbia boast to all the neighbours that her generation build the houses with stone and name the place Yag[5]. Her mother hand it to her that her generation was Yag people because her people came from Yag. She could not explain what Yag was all about. Up to this day, I don't know what Yag means, or if there was such a group of people. Jumbia say massa William call the place New Camp, because that was the first place slaves settle since they leave Nigeria.

I remember that Jumbia use to tell people where Nigeria was. Lady Jumbia use to believe that Nigeria was south of the island of Montserrat, that is twenty five miles southwest of Antigua. She always say that Montserrat blind she yie from staying at Hawksbill and see where she people come from. Up to the time Jumbia dead, the poor soul have not a clue as to where Nigeria or Yag can be found. Back then, the poor people of the village, all of us use to believe that Nigeria was just where Lady Jumbia say it was. The place Jumbia call Yag, the planters in my time, call it Stone

3. Very Tall.

4. A phrase used to describe a person who talks a lot.

5. A small community off the river Niger in Nigeria

Harbour. Some would say Stony Harbour. Any amount of stone is right there. Planter William Abbott live at Stony Hill for a long time. That place was the closest plantation to Yag. Young massa Abbott use to call Lady Jumbia, lady Yag, because she talk about Yag so often. Abbott use to say there was no such place. He never hear of it. My mother call Lady Jumbia the Village Yag. At times she would call her chat-a-box.[6] My mother also would think that she talk plenty sense.

I remember Jumbia saying that the freedom day pass quietly. Some crawl into church for the first time. Many could not believe the Freedom day come at last. They look at one another to make the first move. The thing that pile up in their minds was, 'who would give them food to eat if them left de massa'? 'Who a go help arwe?' Lady Jumbia say her people[7] ask themself the question over and over, a wah dem go do? Her people had not a copper.[8] She explain to us that the closer the day of the freedom get was the harder the future was looking for them. More and more they did not know what to do. Not a man or woman was certain. The slave massas did not know what move the free people would make, and the slaves were not certain of what the massa would do to them.

The ex-slaves would have one thing foremost in their heads, no life could be harder than what they have been through. For well after a year after the freedom bell ring out, most of the free people did not make a big stir. Plenty were like wondering sheep. It did not seem to many as if slavery was all over. Most of them did not even get drunk. They did not know how to take the brand new day. Jumbia keep saying arwe tek long fu feel the argos[9] breeze. Too long fu feel the argos breeze.

People seem to feel the world fall from under them foot.[10] Ex-slaves was told that they could set up house on the Kings land.

6. One that talks a great deal.
7. It will appear that the new freedom left the slaves with no economic security.
8. No money.
9. August was the month that slavery ended, hence the August freedom
10. They have lost everything

The Methodist tell the people at Freeman's Village, that freedom means that they were free to stay with the massa. It also means they were free to leave the massa. As slaves, they could not make decisions. As free subjects they can now make their own minds up. No one could force them to work the Nugent hours, or the Nugent time, or the Nuget labour. According to Lady Jumbia, the Moravians take the lead. The meetings cause a stir. They tell their people that the best thing to do was to live by themself. After that message, the setting up of separate villages start slowly, but surely. Lady Jumbia harp and harp[10] again and again, that she was head of four gangs that help to put up new villages all over the land. She use to say that she remember she work with a Jonathan Paul of Mount Williams and Peter Rudd, a Febie Casey, Dan Crump, one Dodo Smith and a Dada May from Fanchebel. She also talk and talk of a Mandell Colbourne of Parham. She also call names like Ashley Joseph, Nathan Humphreys and Samuel Nibbs. I remember she would tell us of a Freda Mae, a Laura Joseph and Ruth Abbott all of Betty?s Hope. These were just a few of the names I remember she always call. Much more names were in the Methodist note book up to 1954 just before they open the new church. I think that the church people in 1954 feel that the record was too old for them to transfer into the new church. Too much rubbish. They burn them. Or maybe the people never know what they were clearing out and setting on fire. Jumbia always praise up the Methodist and the Moravians. She say she work like son-of-man[11], with church people. But she never make the mistake and attend a church service. She always live and ded that the God, and everything that parson and the priest talk about was against the slaves. Not for them and their picknee. No, not at all.

According to Jumbia, there was a little slow down of the work in 1835, but by the beginning of 1836, the ex-slaves refuse to work the Nugent hours. Man, the ex-slaves was beginning to feel

---

10. To keep repeating the same thing over and over

11. A phrase that was used in earlier times to reflect or describe how hard blacks had to work.

equal to the massa. They begin to decide how and when and where they would work or live.

The Planters find themselves in a bine. They would have to make a move to stop the ex-slave from leaving the estate in droves. Man, massa start to pretend to be doing some nice things. A little more food, some clothing and a few pennies was parcel out to the free people. They increase the days pay and bring in piece - up work[12]. According to lady Jumbia, that move was not enough to hold back the black people on the estates. She would laugh when she relate that the biggest policeman in the land, one Hobble[13] argue that slavery would have to come back to stop the people from leaving the estates. He call the people free dogs. Most free people know this man. The man was a mix breed or what people call coloured. The Warner Plantation people nearly stone him to death. They break-up his horse foot. That cool him off but did not stop him. He go to the governor and tell the governor to ask the mother country to bring back slavery. The ex-slaves he claim was bringing un-call for trouble in the land. The governor put a blind yie[14] to what he want.

Life was hellish for people who go and live by themself. Food was hard to get. Lady Jumbia tell the neighbours that God sea-water rescue them. They make small fish pots out of chink wood or mountain parry wood or guinea wood. Black wither wood and the white wither wood was also used. When I say small fish pots, I mean that the fish pots could be bout two or two and a half to even three feet in length. The width could be anything less or the same. Don't believe that they have boats to take the pots out to sea. Not such a comfort at that time. Slavery left few swimmers. Hardly anybody could swim then. What they use to do was to set the pots around the seashore. At times they may go as far out into the sea as

12. Like in modern times, people were paid by the amount of pieces of work they produced.

13. The correct name for the Chief of Police at the time was Lovell but slaves called him Hobble.

14. The Govenor ignored him,

they could stand up firmly in the water. People use to ketch good enough fish. Not any big big load all at one time but enough to satisfy them.

Just enough for a meal would do. They would set the pots overnight and draw them next morning. They would set them in the morning as well and pull at sun dust, or when they feel like.

The first set of ex-slaves that move away from the plantation, live for a long time with most of their food coming from the sea, the swamp and the mangrove along with whatever they could get otherwise. The new life style that the free people were forced to live, breed a whole tun of fisherman and fisherwoman than any other kind of people in the first twenty or so years after the freedom. I deliberately say fisherwoman. Our people of this age seem to believe that only man can go fishing or make fish pots. Back then, the women make their own fish pots. In those days, there use to be plenty women at the seaside carrying out their pots and looking for anything that they could get to give them picknee to eat. That was the thing! Them woman was tough. The people would also put dog wood bush or congereel bush in the gut to catch the gut fish. That kind of bush drunk them. They could not trespass as they would like at the gutside of massa estate. He would charge them for thiefing and trespassing.

Other difficulties was ahead for our people. The donkey and horse, the main transportation at that time, was hard to come by. Massa nar lend nar sell them his capital transport. Ex-slaves have to find a way out. People had to carry things on their heads, or in their hands. They start thiefing donkey and horse. People would leave Old Road in the deep south at nights and thief a donkey as far away as Parham in the far north of the island. After a time some of the local people get their own donkey. It was still not easy for them. There were no tools for them to use. Thiefing again from the bakkra was just one way out. The Moravian church people provide some tools at low cost. They trust them until they could pay.

As time pass on, the word freedom was on every lip around the place. Almost every name the ex-slaves call have the word free in it. If free could not be in the word, the name would indicate the freedom. So too was the word August - they would pronounce it argas or hargos. They would pronounce feedome for freedom. Despite all the hardships and privation, the bulk of ex-slaves had one determination, that was to go sleep when them like, and wake up when them like.

According to Jumbia, when the group set up the village, Freeman's Village, the women make up this song: Me a one freeman, woman now. Not a man can send me a sleep. Not a man can wake me up. Me under me own roof, Under me own roof, Me shub me own doe. Me shub me own doe. Me a one freeman, woman now, woe, woe a freeman, woman now.

Slavery was always on Jumbia's mind. She would chat about her generation first village. "Freedom na bring yag. Yag a de fuss, Yag a fu me, Yag a fu me, me mooma tell me so". Ever so often, she would put the load on her head and gone to her home at Yag. The same house that her generation left behind. It was of all stones at the place where she tell the neighbours where the first group of slaves put up the first village in the land. Jumbia, I know was one of our good teachers. She prove to me to be one of the best of her time. People use to refer to her as the thin, thin woman that out live the fat ones.

4

TACKLING THE PROBLEM:
Determined to live
a better life.

When MaGregor time was near the end, he give some of the exslaves material to help them put up new quarters. He help mostly those around the town area, mainly from Ottos, Woods and Gray's Estates. His help though, was just a drop in the bucket. He provide them with sil, upright posts, shingles and felt. The felt was for the roof. The people use trash instead on the roof and spread the felt on the floor.

The new shelter was put up without a single nail driven into a wood. That would sound funny to people who do not understand hard times and never have the experience of how poor people have to cut and contrive to make the best out of a bad situation. The exslaves who first went on their own could not buy nail and other building material. That did not stop them from putting up their own shelter. I remember how Lady Jumbia could not tell the measurement of the first set of houses that the ex-slaves put up. She could not understand what people mean when they talk about a yard, a foot, a rod or so. She would show us the size of something by counting her walking steps or the span of her fingers. When she did that, fellow villagers would count the steps or the span of the hand and judge the measurement she would be trying to explain. From how she demonstrate, the regular size of the houses was about eight feet by eight feet. Some would be six by six, and some so small that a big man could not stretch out good in them.

To build the house, the ex-slaves planted the wood firmly into the ground about two and a half feet apart. Flexible branches would then be plaited between the posts. These branches were what we call wattle. They would then tuff [1] the wattle from the inside as well as the outside with trash or grass. The first set of ex-slaves houses were made up much differently to the wattle, and daub houses that some people put up in later years. Some of the first houses were put up without any post planted into the earth. This was a common thing when the earth, where they choose to build, was rocky or stony. They would plait the wattle and tie them up. This type could move.

The interesting thing was how the roof would go on without the use of nails. Back then, the people use a rope they call tar rope. Tar rope was trang [2] just like how nylon rope is trang now. That was the thing they use and tie the rafters to the side posts and anything, else that have to be tied up to complete the shelter.

Who could not get tar rope would use the bark from the manhoe tree. That bark was also trang, trang! The people also use it to tie their animals. They would plant a post firmly in the centre of the house and tie the roof on that post. Wind, the normal ones, could not blow off the roofs. According to Lady Jumbia, not even gut rain [3] could leak the early ex-slave shelter. They were warm,

1. Pack
2. Strong
3. Torrential down pour of rain

49

clean and comfortable fu-so.[4] Stones cover the floor neatly from corner to corner, and was placed a little higher than the level of the land. A trench lead the water away from the house. Those who get no felt would cover the stones with grass. Later, some were able to buy nankeen.[5] They double it up and use it to cover the floor. They did not think of a chair or a bed. Only a cover over their heads was a wish then. Some houses had one window and a door. Some no window, only the door. Tar rope or mahoe bark was the thing they take to make the hinge for both the window and the door. Some doors were not attached to the houses. They tie them on in the night or when the occupant gone out. The people would normally lean them up at the side of the house. The first set of ex-slave houses was put up with the door on the west side. Most of the showers start from the east. The door on the west side was to prevent the rain from down wet up inside of the houses, before they could put up the door when there was a sudden shower.

Some of the first things the people plant for food, was cassava, potato, corn, and pigeon peas. Planting pigeon peas was special. That was for two purposes, fence around the house, and food. The planters tight control prevent the people from getting food to plant as they like. They desperately want the three-month potato vine. That was one of the things that would bring food in the quickest of time. The massas did everything they could to prevent the free villagers putting their hand on that vine that would bring potato in three months. That vine was the saviour for hungry people. All the planters know that. The first three years after the freedom was hard, hard years. A long drought in the same period also add to the suffering.

Despite all the hardship the free people had to face, they were leaving the estates quietly and little by little. They did everything to avoid the mistake that the first set of ex-slaves make when they leave the estate at the sound of the freedom bell. Them that leave first, did not leave with much of anything. They that follow

4. Quite comfortable
5. A cheap cloth.

later did not leave empty-handed. They hold a little money from what the massa pay them. They walk with them cutliss, things to plant and with whatever come to their hands. Lady Jumbia tell the neighbours that her mother sister was a slave at Bellview Estate, but she did not leave the estate until a good number of years after the freedom.

The Moravians and the Methodist tell the people that the money the massa pay them for their work must not be for rum drinking and belly fulling. They must eat fair meals, buy material for shelter and help the church. That was the preaching that make the slaves that did not leave the estates soon after the bell knock, have a penny or two when they leave later.

Some slaves make up their minds to leave the estate but at the same time, give the massa the feeling that they would stay wid-he.[6] Remember, the bakkra want them to stay too bad, so all of a sudden they come lovie-dovie,[7] kind fu-so, but a good number of the free people did not take the bait, after a time.

From all accounts, Ma Gregor was not that helpful to the ex-slave population in general. He did not want to offend the planters and at the same time he did not want to restrict the freedom of the free people. According to Lady Jumbia, he got on as if he a do and till nar do. The thing that help to save the ex-slaves a little was that the massas was frighten. They did not know what the slaves had in mind.

Governor Willie Colebrooke that follow Ma Gregor, tell him "tan-way, real tan-way" [8] In 1838 or so, Colebrooke tell the ex-slaves to settle on any available land. There was where the people start to brok-way and set up their own place like them wild. Coolbrooke was of the idea that the Mother Country could not give the slaves freedom without giving them place to live and a way to make life. He encourage the planters to help them to be decent cit-izens. One of the first massa to heed the call of Governor

6. To stay on the estate with him.
7. Pretending that you love someone when your love is not genuine.
8. The help of Governor Willie Colebrook surpassed that of Govenor Ma Gregor.

Colebrooke was massa Billinghurst, of Hawksbill. He start to sell donkeys to the ex-slaves. Those that have no money, he trust them. He give the three month vine away to the people. Lady Jumbia say one of the best things he ever do, was to give land and material to a group of women healers to build a place to care for the sick at Hawksbill Plantation. The women build that place themselves.

Lady Jumbia say one or two men come round, wet the roof [9] and help them cover it. It always look to me as if there was always something that draw them women healers together. Don't mind the distance, they always seem to find their own kind.

Back then, you could not find anyone easily who would live near Freemans' Village and travel back and forth to Hawksbill or anywhere that side. That don't happen even now-a-days when people have motor and bus to take them as far as they wish. Mark you, that was nothing for Lady Jumbia to do. She ride donkey and sometimes walk from Yag village to Hawksbill, about ten miles or so away, to take care of the sick. My mother used to call her a woman and a-half. A place for sick people is known as a hospital or doctor shop. The women healers stay clear of any name like them so. They just call it de Sick Hark. Back then, the name Hawksbill was not such an easy name to call. Some would pronounce it Harkbill and some say Harbill.

The women healers at the Sick Hark would try almost everything to revive the sick. One have to be seriously sick to escape exercise. The women healers use to feel that when a sick person keep still they encourage death or deeper and longer sickness. Lady Jumbia prize herself as one of the best on rubbing. No woman round the place could rub like me, she used to say. She would show her fingers while she talk. Jumbia say they have two kinds of rub. The five finger rub and the ten finger rub. The five finger rub was to rub with one hand. The more serious rub was the ten finger. That is, to rub with the two hands at the same time. The hands would move like a loco crank shaft, back and forth and up and down the body.

9. To put a flag on the roof and toast to the erection of the house

Whatsoever the sickness, they would rub the bottom foot, rub and exercise the ankle properly, rub the back and place the palm of the hand at the back of the head for some time. The world change plenty since then. Things that happen back then, will always sound like joke to most people now-a-days. Not even the well and strong people today put their bare foot in dew grass. But back then, at the sick Hark, the sick must get up in the mornings and walk on the dew grass when dew fall overnight. This Lady Jumbia tell the neighbours, make the body and limbs move freer. In those days, there was hardly any shoes. People bottom foot was thick and hard. The heel of some people had a split in the centre. Beside knowing what bush to apply and the quantity for different ailment, vinegar was a common medicine at the Sick Hark. As a matter of fact, no woman healer travel without vinegar, turpentine and allumn. Wet a piece of cloth with vinegar and tie the head was one of the first things that happen when someone get sick. It stop bleeding quick, quick. Turpentine was for cuts and bruses. Sugar work give plenty of that.

They would also grow castor leaf. That was to draw out the fever and the oil heal the inside.

The barking of the body was another serious practice at the Sick Hark. That was to boil up all kinds of bush. Dip in as hot as the body can bear it, then soak and wash from head to foot. The barking of the body was done to take away certain pains, laziness and bad feeling. It was also to revive the person when feeling tired and flog out. Women get special treatment when they confine[10] at the Sick Hark.

They make jackstrap for the men and they prepare young gal for the coming of their first monthly things.

They make picknee clothes, bib, head tie and belly band for the picknee and the mother that just confine. In those days, the mother wear belly band for a period of three months or so after the birth of the picknee. I have the belief that one of the things why so many women in this land look overgrown now, is because they do

10. Gives birth to a baby.

not use the belly band anymore. The older heads, old timish. The women had the belief that the belly band help keep the tender muscles together, and prevent them from growing out at will. So much women in my time never get out of shape like the young people I see today. Another thing that I see them do different to days gone by, is that people would eat anything any hour and go to sleep.

That bring them plenty bigger than what they should be. They have to be killing off themselves. Old people can't talk to them. My mother always tell us that we must not eat our belly full and then go to sleep, or go in the sea or pond to wash our skin. Right or wrong, me obey she up to this day.

Nearly all the ex-slaves, use to have very little to do with the Anglican priests and Anglican church people. The dislike was because the slave massas, nearly all of them, if not all, was belonging to the Anglican church at some time. The Anglican priests too, give the slaves a rough time. There was quite a difference to the way the Methodists and Moravians deal with the slaves to that of the Anglicans. After the Anglican priests talk against the prenticeship, some ex-slaves begin to give them some respect in a way.

Some of the Anglican people also get some friendship with ex-slaves after they begin to use the Anglican Meal Society to feed some of them. The Society was there from sometime way back. They run it with money from the Assembly and church collection. Anything Anglican was government. In those days, the Anglican rule the Mother country.

The main work of the Anglican Meal Society in slavery was to help the poor bakkra or other high colour people in the land. Mark you! They use to have rich and poor bakkra. They were not slaves, but dog was better than some of them. A slave massa never want anybody that old and can't work. There was where the Anglican Meal Society use to come in.

The Methodist use to have a place that take care of motherless gals. There was some long and hard search for loved ones after slavery. There was where the big pain was. The Moravian and Methodist parsons joined in the search sometimes. Some was lucky, to find their people. Others walk till them heel nearly drop off. The search go on for years and years. Some people never stop searching for their people. They die searching! The older head say to walk, fool is better than see-dung fool.[11] Some family would be in different islands. Nobody could find them. Some people did not even know the right name of the family member they were trying to find. Different slave masters give different names to the one the slave carry before the sale. Some of the ex-slaves would certainly have difficulty calling the very name of the person for whom they were searching.

One of the biggest regret the planters use to have, after slavery, was that they have very little control over the ex-slaves. A good number of them use to carry, almost daily, a sour face. They cuss the ex-slaves who refuse to stay on the plantation. Anything bad was for them! But the strange thing was that they have trouble with those that stay on the estate after a time. They could not find them to work most of the time when they want them. They too, start to use the freedom to roam the land.

When they leave they were not in a hurry to go back for any set time. That was the hard part. The bakkra could not take that. Neither could they take how the free people face up to them. The ex-slave masters complain bitterly to the Anglican church about the behavor of the free people. One, Massa Redwood from Cassada Gardens, and another one they call Osbourne of Tomlinson, and a big gut bakkra name William Gregaory of Briggins, lead the massas to a Church meeting. The cry was that the lazy dogs kimbo their hands and look brazen on them. When they talk to them bout the work, they go on as if they dont hear a word, and as soon as them talk a little hard to them, they left the work and gone. The planters beg the church to talk to the people. They remind the Anglican church men of the promise they made that the slaves will go be order, that they make Bible oath for slaves, that they will remain and

---

11. To go in search of what you want rather than sitting and waiting for help.

work for their massas. They follow the Moravians and Methodists and rant and rave that prenticeship was not warranted, now everything gone upsided down.

According to Jumbia, the big people in the Anglican Church call in the Methodist and Moravian leaders. I believe, may be that was the first time they talk to them together. They cry about the ex-slaves bad ways and ask them to talk to their followers. At that time, the Moravians have the most followers, then the Methodists and then the Anglicans. The Methodists call the people of the neighbouring places to a class meeting up Freeman's Village Chaple to talk of their behaviour . After one parson done say ee-piece,[12] meeting mash up. Not a soul lend ear to them.

Later in the 1830's and early 1840's, the solution the bakkra find for the shortage of hands was to import wheel barrows, and the hurrow plough. These equipment they feel would take the hands of the absent ex-slave workers.

I always take long and hard to believe that it was the human hands that plough all the land in this place, through slavery, and after. The cattle plough, R.S.D. Goodwin tell me, was brought into the land about three years and six months to four years after slavery. I remember I look at him as if I did not believe him. And he very well know that was what I have in mind. So he look at me and say, "Dumbars have 160 acres and have 200 slaves. There could be no reason to buy a plough? Ample slaves was in the land to work all the land with ease."

The ex-slaves had some falling out with the only people they could rely on a little. Some of the people of the village put up tents and start to hold singing meeting and tea meeting and other meetings in the newly put up villages. The Moravians and Methodists was highly put out. Before the freedom, they control and administer all singing meetings, tea meetings, and any affairs of any kind up to some years after slavery.

---

12. To speak ones mind.

These functions were designed to test how much of the Bible and of the hymn book a person could repeat in words and songs. There was the saying in those days that the church slaves was the brightest. Singing meeting and other things were not for the general slave population. All the talk you hear certain people talk about the church teaching slaves christianity, take it from me, no slave could just leave and go church to hear bout any Jesus Christ.

All the preaching the Moravian and Methodist want to do to slave, they would first have to get permission from the particular slave master to get any of them to church. And if they do let them go to church, the parson was responsible to turn them back into the hands of the massa, safe and sound. The people must remember that the church use to have slaves. I would have to take care that when people talk about preaching to slaves, it could be that they mean preaching to the slaves that belong to the church planters, not the bakkra slaves generally.

Lady Jumbia say that most of the people did not worry with the church people, one bit. They put up wattle tents and hold functions whenever they want. Nearly all of the people who did not want the singing meeting up church, never go to singing meeting until after slavery.

There was a difference between the singing meeting and the tea meeting. Not much big difference anyway. The singing meeting would start a little after midday. They would break and serve food. The tea meeting was a night affair. It would start at seven or eight and people would get tea instead of food. A high up of the church would always chair the function, and would also be the judge. The winners of the church singing meeting or tea meeting, was usually given a Bible or a hymn book for the prize. I want all of you to understand that, for a long time, most of the people who win bible or hymn book, could not read one word out of them. What use to happen, was that these people hear something, learn it and repeat it. That was the story! The church people never believe that any ex-slave could teach Bible verses to anyone. They never expect that the people could get food to share and prize to give out. The free people who want to move the functions from under the control of the church, would soon find out how to control and organize them.

The free people did not care at all whether they could read or not. They recite and sing what they want to recite or sing. They would enter the contest and do not care who would be the judge. They just want to have them own subbon. The church people have the feeling, that only people who could read could judge people. Ex-slave did not understand that. Anybody could be the judge for their singing meeting in the tent. What the winners get for prize could be a yaba, a wash dish, or a jar pot made at Sea View Farm. Sometimes the prize was some food or help to set up a house for the winner. Almost anything could be the prize. Singing meeting and tea meeting for the church, use to take place on Easter, Whit and Christmas Sundays, and some other Sundays in between. The New Year singing meeting could be on New Year's Sunday or the one that follow. The free villagers use to hold their thing much more regular.

The new special date for the function of the free people was the First Sunday in August. Nearly every soul use to get sal-sal at that time. That was freedom singing and talking. People make up their own thing and say them and sing them. They make music with the banjo. They blow the conch shell. They make a sound from bamboo wood or wild cane harrow stalk, or anything they could get to make noise.

Village tent singing meeting and tea meeting become the order of the day. The people used to boast and show off. Even if what they sing or talk did not make sense, it was the pleasure, the jokes, the laughing and the merriment. That was the place where man would go to look a gal, or where man and woman would see if they can get to pair off. Men also get fame to be the best speaker or singer. That kind of fame make them the hero for the place where they live. Gal would love them and war for them.

Lady Jumbia was one of the people that carry the singing meeting down into the village. She did not support the church and the kind of service they keep. Whoever know her, would know that. But she also say the main reason why some man was so much for the functions to take place in the village tent, was because they want to drink grog and harbor what conduct they like.

The other difference in the church singing meeting and tea meeting to that of the free village people, was that of the village would end in dancing. The banjo was the main instrument. The dance after the function was the bottom of the boiler, and would go until cock crow a foreday morning.

The church men always cry out over the new style of the function. Most villagers deaffen their ears to them. The people who follow the church singing meeting could fold their arms when them ready, or clap when them choose and be quiet like lambs as they wish. They were free to do just that. The free villagers too was free to drink them grog and do what they like down in the tent. Well after all, it was the freedom that they were waiting for and after that come, they could die. Another reason why so many people follow the village Singing Meeting and Tea Meeting was that plenty people in this land did not want to get too close to the bakkra church and the bakkra God. Many slaves and some other people in the land, use to have far different belief about God to that of the planters. This only come out clear, after the end of slavery.

The beaten and broken slaves would naturally lean on the parsons for help in slavery time, mortally glad for any kindness from them. But they all know too well that the massa was well offended even if they accidentally get close to the church. Blow for them. Many ex-slaves did not accept or want to hear anything of the God that those priests talk about.

Me think that all the nega people who follow the bakkra religion after slavery, and up to near the start of the 19th century, was just edge up.[13] Want to rub up with bakkra. Play big and better than some people. Nothing else. Plenty of our people like to

---

13. To suck up to another person, group or authority thinking that you will benefit.

shub them head way their body can't pass.[14] A vast portion of the ex-slaves back then, scarcely harbour the thought that the massa God would want to have anything to do with poor people. This old man is at liberty to tell anybody that many people in the early days, become part of the slave massa religion, while deep down in their hearts they disagree with it.

I hold this firmly, because apart from what I see for myself, many old planters like William and George Goodwin and John Foot say the same thing. They always say that if the ex-slaves had just one planter to talk about a next religion other than christianity in this land, soon after slavery, it would make a big difference with the membership of the christian church. The Goodwin family own the front benches in the All Saints Anglican Church. They use to quarrel with some of the planters who would not go to church. It was mostly when he had that type of quarrel, that he would talk about how they were lucky not to have a rival religion in the land.

Lady Jumbia dead before I get to know the Goodwin family. Of course she dead well before they make me a bosom friend. The Goodwins, and many other planters never had anything good to say of Lady Jumbia. They use to curse her everlastingly even though she gone back to mother earth, long time. I had no idea that they know the lady. I learn from George Goodwin that the name was not Jumbia, but Juba; and it is a name from some African tribe.

Massa George used to say she was manny-manny, warrish and ungodly. They usually refer to her as a crane with claws and posses the heart of a hawk. A devil woman they would call her sometimes. They claim that one of the things she used to do was to encourage people to break away from the Mother Country Church. He would continue to say she want people to follow her to build a religion for herself. Sometimes they would add that she was dam lucky that no one out she light. She lucky, she grow old. The Goodwin family though, was honest enough to tell me exactly some of what Lady Jumbia use to tell the village people. Things like the

14. To force yourself into things when you are not wanted.

building of free villages and the many people with different ways of how they pray and worship their own God. I remember how they use to call people foolish and ignorant when they pray to anything other than what they think is the true and living God.

Some ex-slaves use to pray to the rising sun mostly when it was peeping over the hill. They would face the sun with outstretch arms with head bow and eyes shut. Some of them believe that the sun should never rise and meet them in bed unless they were sick and can't move. If they could not move they would do what they can to face the rising sun and pray to it. This was the way the women do it at the Sick Hark down Hawksbill.

The people in the Crabb valley area in the south of the island, would pray when the sun was rising over the Shekerly Hills. Back then, most of the people of Old Road, wait for the sun to come up over the encircling hill of Massa Ruin Estate to pray to it. There was the people too, who believe that any water that spring out of the earth, was holy and could cure disease.

There was people in this land who believe that the right place to meet God, was around springs of water. There were some who would wash their skin in Musette spring and say their prayers right there. A fence was around the spring and no idlers could go close to it. People could not get pass the gate if they were not going to pray. The Musette family that own the Musette estate, did not believe in the God of the planters. The same thing happen at the spring we call Essess hole at North Sound. Some people believe that the painkiller tree at Essess hole get the power from the spring underneath it. That is what cure the pain. According to them, Tom Moore Spring in the South, they claim have the same power.

There were some other people who would go to springs and ponds and have what they call, a muddy wash. The planters call the muddy wash, craziness. To have a muddy wash, was to wash your skin in a pond or the spring, plaster the whole body, from the crown of the head to the soul of the foot with mud, lie down in the sun for up to three or four hours, and then wash the body off in either the pond or the spring. The belief was that all flesh come from mother earth. That there could not be a better thing to cure pain and make people feel better than the earth and its springs of water. The same people believe that God was in the pond and that was why the pond water is warm in the mornings.

This land was a mixture of all kinds of people. It may be too hard to understand it now. There was some who claim that the water running on the earth was the best water to drink. To drink the running water from the overflowing stream or spring running on the earth was the same thing. Most people living in the South of the island use to carry on this practice well pass the beginning of the 20th century. To them, this kind of water was the purest, and will keep them from getting sick. Most bakkra use to think that this water would make them sick and may kill them and Nega people was mortally crazy to drink it.

And still there was another kind of ex-slave that use to practice their religion on a Friday. To the planters, that was so strange and out of all reason. To them, Sunday was the only day to put aside for God. When the ponds dry up, because of the drought, the bakkra pray from his pulpit for rain to come. After slavery, ex-slaves would go to the pond and perform a rain dance. According to Lady Jumbia, she was in the first rain dance that was in the 1830's round Body Pond. She tell us that the rain dance bring the rain. The God rain all afternoon, she tell the neighbours. She also say the rain dance make the rain pour down hard.

There is a cross road in the Anglican Cathedral Church yard. The bakkra people use to go there on special days at the rising of the sun. They spread out their hands so that their shadow form into a cross, right in the cross road. They would make their wish, say their prayers, and do what they want to do. The Goodwins believe that this was in order, because they never suggest that they were praying to the rising sun and not to the Heavenly Father. Mark you, this was a regular thing.

Now I don't see a trace of anything to bring to mind that there were people in this land who think of God differently to the way of the slave massas. Never mind how the thing look ignorant and funny, some of them should be known by the generation that is alive. Tom Moore, Musette and Esses Springs should never close up. I work land at Musette near the spring. The water is cold and salty. There would be more important springs that I don't know about.

Whatever the free slaves use to do, seem to always hat-de-yie[15] of the old slave massa. The big thing that hurt them most was the refusing of the ex-slaves to live and work on the plantation, as if they still own them. The ex-slaves were in hot, hot, pursuit of real freedom. Their oath was never to return to plantation life.

The people who use to live in slavery surely know what the slave life was all about. With that in mind, they were determined to live life how they feel like. Massa never stop planning for them.

According to Lady Jumbia, many massas hate the exslaves that walk away from the plantation. The exslaves she point out was determined to enjoy their freedom. She always say that they were in the front row. And with that in mind she work like the son of man to put up free villages.

---

15. Seem to anoy.

5
PUTTING UP VILLAGES:
Hard work, fun and
love to the Proper

My old ones always talk of how our people use the new freedom in 1834. Many left the estates. Many set up new villages. Some continue to live on the estates. Some live off the estates but work on them. Many fish for a living. Some just don't work again for the massa. Labour shortage was a big concern for the bakkra. Man, this problem was getting real bad because the bakkra could not use the people as they like.

The people that vow they would never cross foot on the plantation to work again for a man that use to own them keep their word. Instead of the people can't bear the pinch and so return to their vomit and live under them it was the bakkra who could not bear the pinch. Could't bear it one bit. They could not have the happiness they were accustom to have unless the poor people was around to shoot the hard labour for them.

Believe it or not the bakkra was well under pressure since the freedom. They twist and they turn to find the answer. What to do to keep the people under them?

The people make life how it comes. They take it with a smile. More and more of them continue to live well out of the sea. Some prople become good swimmers. The little piece of land they were forced to kotch up on, become a capital garden around the yard. Every inch was plant up with some kind of food. People who did not use the pigeon peas plant for the fence, would use the cassie plant. Every body know that cassie is a capital relish. Just to eat boil fish and the peas was enough for them. Sometimes eating peas alone or cassie alone would do. The people properly bear their wants. What they did not have, the exslaves decide to do without. Don't make any mistake people find out long time what the lesson was to live by themself.

That lesson was, rather than knocking up for the Bakkra on his estate, knock up for thyself. Every minute of the day massa pray for something bad to happen to the people. They spread plenty of rumour. As the wind blow the whole place pick up the rumour. One of the big rumour was, the Mother Country was to bring back slavery.

The Bakkra never stop praying to their God to let something bad happen to the people who just won't work for them. While their breast was full to the brim with that prayer, in walk the earthquake of 1843. Man everybody think it was the judgement day that the Priests and the Parsons love to talk bout come. Lady Jumbia say, the massas down Hawksbill where she was, run for their life. The earthquake take place in mid morning. The sea water boil up and bakkra and everybody stay clear of the sea for days. Plenty things crash round them. The earthquake did not do too much damage to the new village houses. Earthquake hardly damage trash houses. Part of the earth under some of them crack up. But that kind of house would ride with the shake.

As usual before the Bakkra cry, the Mother Country rescue

them. The Goodwin family say that the Mother Country send down one tun a money - over quarter of one million pound sterling to them. In those days that portion of money would be more than sufficient to build back the houses, the Mill Towers and do all the repairs and more.

Some of the people who was still living under the massas of Willowby Bay, and Fars Hill, move away and set up the village of Freetown in that same year. The sweetest thing was, while the Bakkra keep mourning over the damage of the earthquake and was afraid of the wrath of another one, the people put up more and more villages. That time the Bakkra get the message very well. When anybody move from under the massa it would be wasting of time to look for them again. No more work they want with them. Bakkra could hardly find anybody that was willing to shoot hard labour for them. Things went from bad to worse.

The massas think of getting people from outside to work the fields. One Massa Jackson of Belmont put to the Assembly that they should bring in East Indians. The other Planters nearly swallow him whole. The Antiguan Slave Massas, throughout slavery dislike Indians regardless where they come from. They then settle on the Massa Shan Plan to bring in Portuguese. I think that it was the year after the earthquake the Assembly pass the law to give themself the right to import Portuguese. I get it from the Goodwin papers that the Governor in the land at the time was not in favour. It was the Mother Country that say if the people of the Colony won't work nothing else could be done. The Mother Country was terribly put out with the people because they won't work in good spirit with their old-time Slave Massas. God make it so that they go and bring in the Portuguese. That was the mistake.

There was the argument that the Portuguese did not work the way the massas expected. Never mine, they were still of great help to the Planters. What they would be able to do along with what they could scrape out of the exslaves that remain on the plantation, would improve the situation. At least that would ease one side of the pressure a little. The planters could hardly get rid of the pressure that they get by not having the kind of people that would shoot the hard labour for nothing. To get labour for nothing and the control, was the real sweetness for the bakkra. Not a-thing sweet them more than that.

Many planters say that the larger number of Portuguese that land here, could read a little. They were always regarded by the Planters to be in a much higher bracket than the Nega-man. The Planters give them respect and by all means treat them better. That cause some contention. It make some of the exslaves that was fearful of moving away from under the bakkra get pluck. At one time, when the Portuguese move in the quarters that the Planters prepare for them, some exslaves would be moving out from under the bakkra at the same time. So if the Planters ever had in mind that importing Portuguese would check the flow away from the estate, they was certainly mistaken.

Some bakkra feel that when the exslaves see that people come to replace them, they would change their minds and hold on to what they could get. I remember my mother say that near the end of the 1840's, there was about close to 40 villages all around the land. Jumbia did not understand clearly what the figure 40 was. How she show us the number was that she count her fingures and toes and we get to understand how much she was talking about.

One of the bitterest slave massas that could be found against the ex-slaves because they won't stay on the plantation was Dick Gregory of Briggins. He was so bitter that at a prayer meeting at the All Saints Anglican Church leading up to the Easter Sunday in 1847, he pray for God to send a hurricane with just enough wind to blow away the trash houses, so that the own-way and senseless vagabonds, would find them way back to their massas. One Parson Jones who happen to exchange his pulpit from St Phillip that Sunday, call Gregory a lunatic. The Goodwins interpret the Gregory prayer to mean no harm. He was just a don-k-dam-man[1] they claim.

1. One who speak or do things without consideration for others.

Throughout the years mostly during the hurricane season, the Planters use to recall with plenty joke, the Gregory prayer. My mother would say big gut Gregory prayer was for all the bakkra. Only after that generation of bakkra dead-out sometime after the turn of the century, the Gregory prayer fade out. That was the joke that last for year upon year- nearly fifty.

Many times throughout life when people wish something good or bad, it happen. It is not to say they would get the wish they want or it will happen exactly as they want it. The people in my time use to take a bad wish seriously. Even if the wish was not all that bad, but that person did not want it, that person would respond mortally quick and would say, na wash no mouth pan me or they would ask with a certain amount of passion and resentment "awah you a wash mouth pan me for?"

The bakkra want a hurricane to come bad, mark you! As I see it, they fraid hurricane plenty more than the poor people. Not just hurricane, but anything that would cause damage and death. The bakkra fraid death whole tun[3] more than ar-we.[4] But at that time Massa Gregory pray for a hurricane to come with just enough force to blow the people back to them. The hurricane would surely straighten things out for them. That was the hope.

In those days, people would just size up that bad weather was at hand. In the hurricane season, they would keep on thinking that it would come when they have not the least thought bout it. People would have an idea of the time of the year when to expect a hurricane. They could not tell where it was or when it would strike. The bakkra usually build his house to stand up to the bad weather.

The people would guess when a hurricane was in the area by observing the behaviour of animals and birds. The birds would fly in large numbers away from the land. Some birds were known as "weather bird." Another sign would come from the fowl. They would gather at one place and cackle every now and then. Cattle would have some unusual behaviour, irritable and run all over the

2. To wish and say negative things.
3. A great deal.
4. Us

place. The donkey would bawl often. The horse was one of the best indicators, they would not move from stable easily, and give plenty of trouble.

People would not take too much chances when they see anything or any unusual sign at anytime of the year, but in the hurricane season, they would surely pay more attention. The people in the villages would do all their business in the churches when hurricane was around the corner. Nearly everybody would bundle up in the Methodist or Moravian churches or buildings. They would not leave until they feel sure that the hurricane would not come or that it had come and gone pass the land. The people on the estates would bundle up in the building they feel the safest. As usual, there would be some people who would play hard headed and nar-move,[5] useless anybody talk to them.

The free people houses meet them first serious natural disaster in 1848. The Gregory prayer come true. Hurricane come and mash up the land, and sweep away nearly all, if not all, the village houses. As a matter of fact, those that remain, were of little use. Briggins gut over flow and carry way nearly all big gut Gregory animals. His house roof blew off and his groom house blow down flat. The Freemans Village Methodist Church book record have in it twenty-one people could not be found in the Colony after the hurricane. My father people did not behold their uncle Marky again. They could not talk enough to get him to follow them to shelter at the Freeman's Village Chapel. And they find Kunky Jonas body over at Cedar Hill gut fasten between trees. Death can be the price for hardeness.

The massas did not well cry for help before the Mother Country lend a hand. They could shut them yie and depend on her. She always treat them good. The village people was like them loss, well shaken up. The Planters see that and start to sweeten them up. They were in such a state that the Planters feel that was the time when they would go back to them. Fulfill truly, the Gregory prayer. At least for a while, this was the thinking and the hope. The weath-

5. Real stubborn.

69

er beaten and homeless ex-slaves would be glad to return under them. This did not happen. The pleasantest thing that ever happen, say Lady Jumbia is that them massas could not sing sweet enough. The people return to nothing and rebuild their homes. They were prepared to weather the storm.

Lady Jumbia use to relate the story again and again about the Gregory prayer. I always use to keep thinking that I see the Slave massas with them mouth wide open and could not say a word. Shock! Dumfounded , and could not believe what they saw. Some of the massas put up houses a little way from the main estate nega house and give the people permission to live in them. Do you believe this? The Goodwins say the people refuse the offer.

Fear of too much freedom to ex-slaves was a growing concern for the bakkra. Antigua use to have a newspaper they call Antigua Weekly Times. The bakkra refer to that newspaper as the Roll Call. The Goodwins say a year or so after the hurricane, the paper sound the warning that the attitude of the ex-slaves will bring disaster on the land. The paper call on the Mother Country to protect the massas and family, if not, the time will surely come when those vagabonds will take over the land.

The Gregory prayer did give plenty strength to the people. They even make-up this bena.

> *Ar Massa Gregory dis a fu-me*
> *Dis a fu-me, Dis a fu-me*
> *Me go tretch out in dey*
> *Dis a fu-me, Dis a fu-me.*

And they would add any amount of words with the chorus, sometimes bad wod[6] too. And as they put back up the houses, they would carry on.

> *Dis a fu-me, Dis a fu-me.*

And they would carry on and on and on.

6. Expletives.

When I was a boy, I use to believe that nobody know about the village more than Lady Jumbia and my mother. The surprise was when I meet George Goodwin. He know most things. Through him and the village old people, I get to know more about some of the villages and where they were located.

A man, Scotland of the Free Press and the Methodist along with the Moravian keep telling the ex-slaves that William Wilberforce and another man name Clarkson help to fight plenty for their freedom. The people could not call the name Clarkson. They say Cockson. They believe that he was a trang man. Box dung[7] anybody. Tump you dung[8] as you wink. In those days, when someone was playing a bully, they would call that person a Cockson.

There was the village name after William Wilberforce. They call it Free Wilbour. That was just south of Parham on the hill between Parham and Parham Hill. Immediately west of Free Wilbour was the one they name after Clarkson. They call that Village Free Cockson Village. The Moravian and Methodist big people name most of the villages, but some of the ex-slaves use to run race to name village also.

West of Parham Hill, was Free Deliliah Village. One of the man that help put up the houses get so drunk after they wet the roof of the first house, that he fall asleep and a woman name Feebie cut off a bunch of his plait hair. The people liken the incident to that of Deliliah and Sampson in the Bible and with that, they call the village Free Deliliah Village.

The ex-slaves of Blackman estate use to make whistle out of bamboo or wild cane. They also use the whistle to make music. That was the way they celebrate first of August. They call their village Free Whistle Hole Village. They would set up on 31st July and blow the whistle to welcome the First of August, year in, year out.

After the freedom the people set up villages all over the land. Man it was real freedom. There was the village they call August North and another that was August South. August North was near

7. Exert physical punishment with an open fist.
8. Exert physical punishment with a closed fist.

71

the sea where the U.S. Navy Base is right now. That is on the north
sea point of the land. August South was south of Winthrope Estate.
That is where the U.S. Army Base is at the present time. So you
would understand that August North and August South were neighbours. There was also the village they call Augusta North and
another one Augusta South. Augusta North was close to the sea at
Boons Point and Augusta South was on the hill south of Boons
Point.

There was the village they call Free Born Village. That was
about half mile north of All Saints Anglican Church. People later
call the same Village Hyman Village. A woman name Gussy choose
the spot for the first house.

The ex-slaves of Montrula put up their village half a mile or
so west of the All Saints Anglican Church that is, on the northwest
side of Montrula. The people call that village Free-Fu-All. There
was also the village that was about three quarters of a mile east of
the All Saints Anglican Church. It was just a little away from where
we call McPond now. And that village also have the word "all" in
it. The reason come from the name of the Church. The people
name that village All Free Village. I think that people now-a-days
should understand how the people back then come up with certain
words. Free Breeze Village was south of Sea View Farm on the hill
that is part of what people now call Emerson Estate.

Freewill Village was north of Sea View Farm on lands now
call Light Foot Estate Freeland Village was on the north side of
Buckley Estate where people now call Olivers.

Freedom Village was south of Belmont Estate, Free Pardon
Village was set up on lands belonging to Ottos Estate east of the
Holberton Hospital near what people now call Merican road. The
word "free pardon" was another word people use to use all over the
place then. The Slave massas have it to say that it was a free pardon for all given by the Mother Country. That was the reason for
the name of the village. Free people Village was exactly at the tam-

bran trees at the entrance of Cedar Grove from the south side and Freeda Village was put up on the hills west of Weatherills Estate.

There was the Free King Village next to Mount Williams and Freehand Village where we now call Brooks Estate and Table Hill Gordon is right where Freefield Village was.

Freelodging was northeast of Parham close to the end of the north eastern tip of the land near to the sea, where Lodge plantation was.

I am not able to say the exact location of many villages in and around Bendals area, but there was quite a few villages that were formed from the estates around. The people put them up sometime between 1839 and 1852. There was Free Winny Village name after a woman they call Winifred. Free Drammie Village, Lady Jumbia tell us that Drammie was a late slave that his mother say come from the Old Goat and he call the village after himself. In later years, George Goodwin tell me that the name is not Drammie but it is Quamie and it is not Old Goat as people have it. It is Gold Coast. And so he would straighten out names that people use to call wrong all the time. The right name of the village then was Free Quamie. There was the Free Jack Spania Village near Warner. The freedom was long in coming and the old people who live to see it compare themselves with a breed of fowl that had little bit of feathers but was a very strong breed. That breed normally out live them with plenty feathers by far. And the saying of the people in the area was, Jack Spania say, "Pray for long life not for feathers." So although the freedom was so long in coming, God hear their prayers and help them to live to see the day. That was why the people near Warner give the village that name. In that same area was the villages Happy East and Happy West. And Sharpo Village, called after the man Sharpe that was with Wilberforce, who labour to free the slaves. Where we now call John Hughes and Sawcolts was known as Coco Valley because of the Coco that use to grow there. The ex-slaves name the place Free Coco Village.

The free people of Betty's Hope set up their village and call it Hopeful West. This village was just west of Betty's Hope Estate. Those of Cotton Estate call theirs Hopeful East. Cotton Estate is about one mile northeast of Betty's Hope Estate. The Codrington family own both estates, sometime ago.

The slaves use to think that James Scotland, the mouth man of the Free Press, was for them and so the slaves at Briggins name their village after him. They call the village Katch Free Village. Most people today would say the right thing, Scotch Free Village. That village was just north of Belmont Estate. The people put up the village south of Bolans estate and name it Free Roses. They that live at a place call Valley name the village Free Valley. Futher south of Bolans was the village call Victory Village and going further south were the villages they call the Victorias. Victoria North was just before reaching Crabb Hill and Victoria South was on the hill overlooking the Crabb Valley Estate. Victory, Victoria, Victor and name like those spring up after the new queen of England get on the throne and carry the name Queen Victoria. There was Free Sunshine Village a little away from the Moravian Church at Old Road and Freedom Valley Village would be half a mile east of the Free Sunshine Village down in the lower part of that area. Lady Jumbia use to live and dead that her generation was the first to put up the village Yag when they come to the land long time ago. The plantain sucker must follow the root. That is the reason why she should live to help to put up villages all round the land. The villages was going up one after the other.

For many years after the Freedom and up to the 1940's or so, a baby born on the First day of August, was counted as a special picknee. This was not a joke. Nearly everyone would take note of that special picknee. They use to call the picknee the Free Born picknee. For the ex-slaves, the month of August was the big, big month of the year. People use to try to get names that would sound closest to August to name a new born. Annette, Augustine, Aggie, Augusta, Arding, Augustus, Agneta and it goes on and on.

Sometime in the 1840's, the slaves loosen up themselves,

they start to spree. Plenty of them have no limit with that. They begin to go in good numbers to the Fig Tree Hill and the Uooge Hill area. A little away from Uooge Hill become the spot for our people. That was the exciting place. Nearly all the slaves in this land hardly know of Fig Tree Hill or ever put foot there. The bulk of them that happen just to hear the name would never know what it was like. Some would pass by and would not even know what they call the place. Whatever cause it, there comes the time when the people start to flock in the area like hive-a-bee.

Back then, the young people always want to brag that they climb over the hill. Some just go to see, but would never venture to walk up nor down. If they come from the west end, they would stay at the bottom and if from the east, they would stay right at the top. When parents find out what the hill was like they use to have their hearts in their hands when their younger ones left home to walk over the Fig Tree Hill. It was the feeling that once anybody slip, right into the water below they would sure to fall and would end up with some part of them broken, or that would be the end of them.

Plenty people use to gather at the area at Easter time and Whit. But the thickest gathering was on first of August. That was the happy crowd. The number use to start gather in from the night before the 1st of August. The place would be pack and busy, particularly when the time come round on the moonlight night. Most people would stay around for more than a day. They would lie down under trees or in make-shift shelter. The trees around was much thicker than now. The people would walk with food to cook, and they would share what food they have with others. They did not have to know the man or woman to feed them up to the proper.

And it was not just eating and drinking alone but wash tun-a-music. There was the drums and anything that could make music. John Bulls use to dance two times in the year. First of August and at Christmas time.

There was plenty of games too. Man in those days, use to

love to show how trang them be. The trangman from the villages would challenge one another in a play fight or, people would look for their match, and "play fight"[9] with them. There was a grip they call the neck arm grip. When a trangman hold a man in that grip and he can't get out, he would just clap the man on his shoulder or side. That was the surrender. The winner would get plenty food from everybody. Sometimes the play fight turn to a real fight. People had to part them and stop the fight.

There was two kinds of eating race. One would be for those that can eat a number of dumpling or potato fastest. Another would be for those that can devour the most food. Sometimes they may eat too much. My mother say, one year, Duddy Lemon, a man from Highman Pasture drop dead after he win the eating race.

Another game was the throwing of stones. The farthest thrower was the winner. And there was the tug-a-war. Plenty people use to love that. Women use to love to pull against men. Some man would never pull against a woman. They get shame if the woman pull them over. Not all times they would have rope. Maho bark was the thing they use most. Sometimes they have to use the heavier kind of wist. Wist was not that strong and would bust and send them tumbling back.

The young and the adventurous would have walking race up or down the Fig Tree Hill but not many would be in that. Think of any form of merriment that people use to take pleasure in doing. Believe it or not, it take place in the Fig Tree Hill area on the biggest day of the year, August 1st.

People use to have it to say that the spot was the quietest and coolest in the whole land. The saying was, when the poor people want peace in their souls, the God send them to the Fig Tree Hill to sleep under the shade.

The people call the bridge that join Uooge Hill and Fig Tree Hill together, "Bridge-A-Peace". They use to believe that to be at that spot would bring wonders to them. Lost friendship would

9. Wrestling.

return. Even lost love between man and woman would get back tight,tight.

When some man and woman fall-out and want to make back up, they would meet right there. In some cases, the man would travel from the top of Uooge Hill and the woman from the bottom of Fig Tree Hill and they would end up on the bridge. On First of August, when the crowd was thick, somebody would always blow a conch shell, a wistle or what they get and call on people that have contention to get on the bridge. The drum would beat for them that find themselves there. Don't go on the bridge or near it if you don't want to dance. Young and old in this land love them dancing plenty. But dancing on the Bridge-A-Peace have a different meaning. That was the real freedom dance.

People today, can only think of this to be a crazy idea. But my mother use to say the Fig Tree Bridge-A-Peace put many man and woman back in love. Say me old Sammy say, that most man would do anything to get a woman to love him. The real freedom was when the people were at liberty to roam the land, meet, fall in love, fall out, make back up with a woman, work when them feel like, spree when they like and live where they choose. Remember that they could dare not do this during slavery. People roam the land, and enjoy the place. Something, they could never do before the freedom come. Me Papa Sammy say those in charge of the land should not destroy the Bridge-A-Peace. They should carry on the custom.

6
TOTAL CALAMITY:
The Grandeur of Hawksbill faded

Lady Jumbia, my old ones and the Goodwins told me of the harsh condition brought on our people just before slavery end. They repeated over and over that it was the hardest they can remember our people have to work since they were born. They could not do a single thing to satisfy the massas. Plenty slaves dead from over work and lack of medical attention. They have to shoot hard labour right down to the stump. Massa want every ounce of blood for the last.

John Billinghurst, the massa of Hawksbill estate, was one of the very few bakkra who did not try to get blood out of stone from his slaves at the time. Jumbia say that as far as she know the Billy family was different. His slaves get some ease during the period when everybody else want the last drop of blood. Some slave owners have it to say the Billinghurst family was the cause for some slaves to believe the rumour, that the Mother Country grant the freedom earlier but the owners was hiding it from them.

The Warner massas put the blame for the slave revolt that take place near the end of slavery squarely on the shoulders of the Billinghurst family. They accuse them of playing up with slaves. The play up give way to the unfounded rumour. The Billinghurst family did not change their attitude to the slaves despite the accusation put gainst them. The Hawksbill plantation flourish.

I don't know how Hawksbill estate could come to be so forgotten. It is nearly some forty years or so that I have not heard a thing about it. Plenty things use to take place on that estate. To me the Hawksbill ground should rank as one of the most historic places in this land. Back then, it was always in the spotlight. There was a phrase a time ago, "To brok tru Antigua, first brok tru Hawksbill". The planters have it to say every shot fired at this land fire at Hawksbill first.

That was the place where the earlier inhabitants make most attacks on the English. Some French people also come in and light fire and burn out Hawksbill. They take over the land for a little while. That was in the 1660's. There was another attack of fire at Hawksbill in the early 18th century by the French and again in the 19th century. After that there was another fire of unknown origin. At Hawksbill there was the Irish "hengman stone". A big stone that was the platform for the gallows on which the English use to hang slaves and Irish people when they ketch them joining with the enemy. The stone was under a turpentime tree. They use the tree to tie on the rope and would just push the man off. Don't mine who the enemy against the mother country, the Irish man was with them.

According to most planters, the Irish would link with the French and cause distress at Hawksbill again and again. So when they ketch them no sparing take place. People say Hawksbill got the name because of the shape of the rock. Some people say that the rock got the name because it shape like a sea turtle that has a mouth like that of a hawk and with its back and head out of the water that make it look like the turtle itself. Others argue that the name come from the flying chicken hawk itself. But whatever the reason for the name the rock is a land mark for the land. Hawksbill was the central point for people that live between Pearns Estate on its south side and Yepton on the north.

Immediately north of the Hawksbill Rock was Landing Bay, one of the busiest slave markets of the land. Further north was Nedds Bay, then Gaud Point, followed by Galley Bay. North of Galley Bay is Deep Bay Point, after Deep Bay Point is Deep Bay itself. Then the Goat Hill war look-out. That is at Cripplegate Throne Bay. The Salt Pond that supply the land with salt all through the years was northeast of Cripplegate Bay, then Pillar Rock. Immediately north is Lablaliah Bay & Lablaliah Point, still going further north is Ballast Bay, Side Hill and onward north of that is Union Bay then Week Point followed by Green Bay.

On the south of Hawksbill Rock, is Gulf Point and south of Gulf Point is land that was belonging to massa Pelecon, owner of the Pelecon Mill that people claim to be the best in the area at one time. Massa Pelecon rename Hawksbill Rock, the Pelecon Rock. That new name slip away after a time. Further south was the famous St. Georges Bay and St. Geoges Estate. The St. Georges Estate get famous for the hefty cattle that the estate use to keep. St. Georges use to name the sturdy looking animals after kings and queens and other big people from England. Fullerton Point is next to St. Georges Bay. Further south is Cold Point, followed by Battery after which is Pinchin Bay and Pinchin Estate and then Pearns Point. Pearns Point is a narrow strip of land that hang out into the sea. At the end of Pearns Point, are five little islands that they call the Five Islands. The Goodwin family record book state that the largest of the five islands loose a large chunk of land from the earthquake in 1843. Piece of the narow strip of Pearns Point also drop off into the sea. Two estates southeast and east of the Hawksbill Rock carry the name Five Islands. There was the upper Five Islands Estate and the lower Five Islands Estate. The village Five Islands as we know it today was never a village. That was the place where the massa of the lower Five Islands Estate build the nega houses for their slaves. This generation would surely believe that people name the village after the five small islands out in the sea. That is far from the case. After the dismantling of Lower Five Islands estate the people did not move out of the nega houses and the name Five Islands remain.

Hawksbill was the capital of the estates north and south of the rock. I learn from many planters that Hawksbill was the home of politics in this land because the First House of Assembly was at Hawksbill in 1649 and the governor use to live in a room in the House of Assembly. I learn too that the House of Assembly carry on there until the French burn it down during the time when they run over the land. At Hawksbill too, was the main market for that area once upon a time. Maybe it could be for the whole island. It is not just now that people from the other islands have been going back and forth selling things. People from the island of Dominica start to bring goods to the land sometime after the turn of the century. Before then was the people from Montserrat, St. Kitts and Nevis. For long years the planters, not poor people, go back and forth swapping their vegetables for meat, and fowl, rum and sometimes coal from the Hawksbill market. Pinchin Estate, the people use to say, make the best Speak easy[1] at the time. It was on a swing for some time. Any amount of meat was at Hawksbill. It was the chief cattle estate. Had the right for a long time to import livestock and supply some of the Estates with all the cattle they want. Back then Hawksbill spread a little over 160 acres or so, was small and rocky; did not produce much sugar cane. It had two jetties. One to land animals and the other to land other goods. This was so up to well past the turn of the century. I am not so sure of the time when the Hawksbill estate stop importing animals. I think it was sometime during the first World war.

To land cattle was a thing I use to stand up and watch with all me heart. I never see more wild and butting cattle in my life. They would jump off the boat straight into the water and head for shore. A fence prevent them from swimming to any other place but

---

1. A home-made rum.

to the shaft. They could not get out, don't mind how wild and fierce they were. Planters lasso them, tame them, and set them to work.

Lady Jumbia always say that the people use to show up what their hand could do at Hawksbill. There was hardly another place in the land that had more crafty people. They could work well with their hands. For generations a particular family use to mould[2] the features of people. When it was not mould it was painting or shape out of wood. When boats pull up from the islands, some sailors use to make sure they get their features shape up in mould, paintings or in wood. That was big business at Hawksbill. When some of the planters decide to get married they use to get the features of the bride and groom well moulded or painted. This was a natural gift between the Hector, the Radison and the Goodall family. It is a strange thing today that no one hear about Mandy Hector, Victor Radison or Countis Sebastian or Blassom Goodall of Hawksbill. Don't mine how good a man be in this land, nine days after he bury nobody remember him. A man don't even have to be dead, just come old and out of sight. In this land out of sight mean out of everything. These people that I tell you about could do anything when it comes to drawing and making of image of people. Some people today go on as if the generations before could not do anything. Me sorry for them. I know Mandy Hector and Blassom Goodall. Massas George Goodwin and Affie Goodwin dead left their image in their bluff that was done by those two people. It was Lady Countis Sebastian and Mandy Hector that draw the plan for some of the great houses including Camacho great house at Millars Estate. And not a copper them get.[3] Piece of bread or bun and some bebitch make them feel good. In those days they feel the work make them friends of them massas. Not thinking about money. And where they learn to draw, only God knows. They never darken[4] a school door yet. Up to now, no woman come up like Lady Countis with she drawing and she could do most things.

2. Clay.
3. Money.
4. Never attend school to learn the art.

The Hawksbill area was popular too because Missy Mabel use to make soap and hot pepper sauce and pepper powder. Most people use to make their own pepper vinegar. Miss Mabel pepper vinegar tell for everybody else, tan-way. None could match hers. The big planters clamour for her pepper sauce and pepper powder. Don't mine who try to get the secret they could not try hard enough. The secret how she make the soap and pepper sauce or pepper powder was for only the family. When she and Countis Sebastian dead out the secret for both soap and pepper sauce dead with them. Not one outsider did they make the mistake and teach. Sometime after they dead-out, I think it was after the First World war, a man name Darcel Radison from the same area begin to make soap. We use to call the soap Racy soap. He was open. He show how fever grass root could give the soap a sweet smell.

There was the Hawksbill comb. Mostly when comb get scarce as everything else, one Norris Billinghurst use to produce the Hawksbill comb. He would cut a piece of wood six to eight inches long and use half the portion as handle and drive nails in the other half. A simple comb for poor people. The comb made out of wood and nails by Norris Billinghurst was soon all over the land.

The Hawksbill rock was a beautiful place during the time that the Billinghurst family was massa of Hawksbill Estate. It was well taken care of. Just like how the planters make slaves change barren rock into glowing sugar cane land, the Hawksbill massas at one time turn the Hawksbill Rock into a beautiful flower garden.

On the rock was the hibiscus, the bouganvilla, the snow-on-the-mountain flower, the red pointsetter and the yellow candle. The reason was to brighten the rock mainly at Christmas time. They also put hurricane lamp to give light between the flowers at the height of the Christmas season. Lady Jumbia use to tell the neighbours that the estate bakkra in the Hawksill area would begin to decorate their houses twelve days before Christmas day and the massas was careful to take them down by midnight, twelve days after christmas. Later than that, she say, would run the risk of hav-

5. People with big belly.

ing bad luck for the rest of the year. The massa never skylark with that.

Hawksbill was a busy spot. A jetty was in line with the Hawksbill rock. A pantoon was between the rock and the jetty. And the drinking and the spree would be on the pantoon. This would happen at various seaons but mostly in the Christmas season.

Back then people have it to say that all dun gut people come from Hawksbill Estate. They use to eat plenty meat. The Billinghurst family did love to spree. The saying was "You think you love spree?". "See Massa Billy." There was a planter name John Entwistle people call him Johnny Whistle. He use to bawl water out his eye when the fete get to his head. He use to bawl and bawl and his chorus was "It is a pity that man have to die." But many planters say not even he could compare with the Billinghurst family. The Billinghurst use to kill for the Christmas meal the male animals that were born nearest to the last Christmas. The animal would be cattle and pig whatever the number that satisfy the feast. Their feast would start well before that of any bakkra in the land and would be the last to end. Some of the Bakkra in the Hawksbill area use to have a special dance to welcome the start of spring. The young Bakkra Missis also would put on a new frock to welcome the start of spring. This they claim was to encourage a new and better start in their life. Lady Jumbia say they use to call the first day of spring, New Day. The Hawksbill fun House was the top entertainment centre in the land for nearly forty years or so. There was three top houses at the Hawksbill Estate. The Great House, the Fun House and the Leap House. There was a passage way that lead from one to the other.

A Great House is not a strange or new thing, neither the Fun House. The strange thing for me was the Leap House. I take a little while to understand it. When Lady Jumbia use to tell the neighbours about it I use to think it was just a joke. After I come man and hear planters talk about it, I could not resist. They usually do with great laughter. Back then, Hawksbill and the surrounding estates use to take care of what they do on a leap day and also what happen to them. Young bakkra missis use to gather together and throw up flowers on the leap day. Who ever ketch the flowers they believe stand the chance of getting married in quick time or some good luck was sure to follow her. The Bakkra usually have a special party all over the place on the leap day, young people mainly the gals would make their wish.

Every leap year at midnight on the 28th February the Bakkra them at Hawksbil have a thing where young people get a chance to pick somebody that would eventually become a wife or a husband. The building in which that use to take place was the place they call the Leap House. It was the custom for many young people to try their luck at the Leap House to find a partner on the Leap Day.

Some call it "Leap Pon Me," others call it Ketch The Leap. The young bakkra family look forward for that special time every leap year. The number of man must out number the gals by one. The young people hardly know each other before 28th February. On that day they would first get their belly full. Plenty food from the Chief Planter of Hawksbill. The dress for the woman kind was blue and white. The people claim that the gals know not a man and the blue and the white mean that them virtuous. Me learn from the Goodwins that they use to call the blue and white Holy Mary dress. At the Leap House the young men would be on one side and the gals on the other. A dark screen separate them and also blind fold them. Once they enter the Leap House they could not see each other. Under a dim, dim light, the drum would strike up minutes to midnight and was sure to stop at the stroke of midnight. The drum beat heavier as they were coming to the stop. Immediately as the drum stop, the young people leap from behind the screen onto a partner. The Leap take place at the same time the leap day of the year 29th February start. At least one man would be left without a gal. He would be the unlucky fellow and would move with speed out of sight. It was the belief that bad luck would follow him for some time. No second chance at the Leap house. The lucky pairs would move from the Leap House to the Fun House where they usually dance till broad morning. Next thing parents and friends present them with flowers and plan for the wedding would begin without delay. And there was the saying - Leap House wedden never spoil. Most people today open their mouth wide wide, when they hear bout this Leap House wedding. Me use to do the same thing. But almost everybody in this land know of Dr. Bailey the Chief Medical Officer for quite some time. In the 1940's he see a woman picture in a London newspaper, fall in love with the picture, and - send for her and married she. Only death part them.

Hawksbill also have lots of badness. Around the Hawksbill area young gals use to disappear more than any other place in the land. Dung dey min tick.[6] Quite often in those days after slavery, young gal would go missing. Particularly those that live on estates near the seaside. Again and again the womankind would just vanish. Gone for good. That frighten everybody round the place. Nothing but pain and sorrow on the mothers and friends.

When the gals them go missing don't mind how people look for them, high nor low, not a trace. No friendly eyes behold them again. Lady Jumbia tell a story of a woman name Ma Dudie from upper Five Islands estate. She use to help out at the Sick Hark. This lady was not one of the greatest woman healers. Her gift was to make clothes. A Moravian woman. Lady Jumbia, use to say that she was one of the very best in the land at that time. She learn the fine points of the trade from the moravians that use to have a tailor shop to teach people how to make clothes.

People have it to say that she was the first ex-slave woman to make shirts for Bakkra. Woman was not allowed to make clothes for man at that time. But she was the clothes maker for the Billinghurst family. She could sing plenty, play the banjo and was one of the woman that keep the surroundings lively. After a time she plait her hair all backwards and tie all the plait together with a white string. She claim that was to send the message to all man that she done breed out she latter. She don't want any more man. Time to

6. The area was bushy, dark at nights and dreary.

rest from man. Women who believe that they have enough picknee follow Ma Dudie hairdo.

After Ma Dudie finish with she sewing she would play her music. She was always up and around. She also use to amuse the Billinghurst when they have their fetting. One particular Saturday, she was not around.

Her family did not know where she lead to. That was rather strange and frightening. - She was not so young. According to Lady Jumbia, a bosom friend of Ma Dudie, she use to keep herself looking rosy. Almost everybody in the neighbourhood went searching for her. High nor low, no Ma Dudie. At that time, she had just four picknee and she mean that she would not have any more. The people then think that she was funny when she make up her mind that she have enough. Four picknee was likkle[7] bit in those days. Likkle bit you hear me. The thinking then was more picknee more riches for the future.

The whole place was in mourning for the loss of the old sweetheart. Some people think that she drown in the sea when she go to draw her fish pot. But that would be unusual. Lady Jumbia say that woman usually have company when they go to set and draw fish pots. At that time the seashore round the Hawksbill area was generally quiet. Sandy Island and Hurst Shoals on the south and Wreymouth Reef on the north keep the water still. Not a ripple most times. The bay was not too deep. The people come up with all kinds of suggestions of what may happen to her. After a complete week past and there was no sign of her some of the villagers believe that shark pull her into the sea and eat her or she dead some how or the other. Some of the Hawksbill people keep up her wake. But one of her bossom friend a woman name Dadda Pinny was mortally vex with them that keep up the wake.

Ma Dudie, Lady Jumbia and Dadda Pinny was pease in a pod.[8] The people use to call them de Happy Three. Dudie use to

7. At that time the average family was nine or thereabout. Therefore four was considered a small amount.
8. They were like inseparable twins or very close friends.

play the banjo at the Sick Hark. The people then use to believe that quiet banjo sound help keep the pain out of the mind of sick people and also set them to sleep. The banjo woman was important at the Sick Hark. The woman they call Dadda Pinny had a natural gift too. Dadda Piny use to tell things that would hapen. She would also let them find people who thief bakkra subbon or do wrong in a secret. Massa Billinghurst family love her. They treat her like a queen because she would tell them where to find things and who steal and who do what. She would tell them what to expect. She would keep them straight in many ways. Best coffee woman. Massa Billinghurst family hardly make a move without Dadda Pinny. She was the all in all for them. The Bakkra call her Queeny Pinny. She was so close to the Billinghurst family that they allow her to feed their dogs. That make she could enter the bluff when she like. That tell the kind of power she use to have over the bakkra. It was a strict rule mortally strict, no man could throw a bone to the Bakkra dog and get way with it. A dog will wink tail to any one who feed it. That means who feed the Bakkra dog will become a Bakkra friend and a friend of the Bakkra dog. That was never to happen at any-time. The Bakkra would kill that dog if it become a friend of a slave or ex-slave. The Bakkra would be completely out of his mind to allow his servant back in those days to have anything to do with his dog. His dog must always be barking with tail stiff out and ready to bite poor people. It was not so with the Billinghurst. Dadda Pinny was the most trusted woman for them. Their dogs and she use to be good, good friends.

Dadda Pinny was vex, vex over the wake they keep up for her friend Ma Dudie. Pinny live and dead that Dudie was still alive because she did not see Ma Dudie jumby.[9] If she was dead she would be bound to see her or something would tell her so. Lady Jumbia tell the neighbours that Dadda Pinny go to a quiet place in the bush near the seashore all by herself. For a whole day she keep way from all the talks about the missing woman. And I remember Lady Jumbia have the neighbours speechless and in disbelief when

9. Spirit.

88

she say that after Pinny come back she tell the Billinghurst that Ma Dudie is not dead. She gone away on a boat and that they tie her hand and foot. She was in a wall near the sea and that she may soon dead.[10] William Billinghurst son of John Billinghurst was the keeper[11] for two of the gal for Ma Dudie. Because of that friendship the Billinghurst family was prepared to do anything to help. The Billinghurst believed that it was Nelson's Dockyard Dadda Pinny was talking about. The Billinghurst family get the boat they call Lady B and with some friends along with Dadda Pinny off they sail to Nelsons Dockyard.

Nearly all the planters in the land back then were soldiers. Ready to fight anyone for the Mother Country. John Billinghurst was a top man at the Dockyard for some time. He was also a big man in the land. Few bakkra in those days could say that they did not know him. Some would gone and others would loose touch with the happenings at the Dockyard because there was no enemy to fight over a long period.

When Massa Billinghurst boat get close to the dockyard, Pinny tell her Massa that was the place she see Dudie in she sleep. As they reach, the Billinghurst father and son leave the boat and go into the baracks to search for Dudie. Lo and behold there was Dudie and five more women tie around the waist to a post and with chain on their foot. Lady Jumbia say that the Billinghurst chop the rope with their cutlass but had nothing to unlock the chain from Dudie foot. They lift up Dudie with the chain on her foot and take her to the boat. As they were about to leave a second thought hit them. They should go back for the others. When they get Dudie no one was around. When they return to loose the others there was the guard and he ring the bell. Ringing the bell at the Base out of time would signal that there was an intruding enemy. That means that all soldiers must leave where ever they may be and report to the Dockyard or to any fort closest to them. Soldiers rushed to Base. They happen to know John Billinghurst. The guard had no choice

10. The fortune teller is trying to explain that Ma Dudie had been kidnapped.
11. A married person engaged in an extra marital relationship.

but to ring the bell. He could not allow him to carry away the women. In the name of the Queen he commanded them to give up the key to the chain. When he get the key he did not unlock the chain. He cut the rope from the post and his men lift them up and carry them to the boat just like how they take Dudie. The boat could not carry the additional people. They had to make two trips. John Billinghurst take the women with the chain on their foot and rope around their waist straight to the Governor for him to see for himself. He must know what was going on at the Dockyard. Massa Billinghurst then set sail for Hawksbill. When the People see Dudie they could not believe. Everybody go pon them spree.[12] All praise to Dada Pinny. The God for Massa Billinghurst and now for all Hawksbill people.

The villagers play music to welcome her back. Everybody was happy. And the story of Lady Jumbia was that Dudie tell Massa Billinghurst that she go to cut wood to make fire to cook as usual and her picknee was to join her but before she reach, out walk a man from the cane field and tell her to follow him. Before she could say anything he tell she to drop the cutlass and out come two other man from the bush. She follow them and they help her on a boat that was near Pinchin Bay and the boat sail way with she. They tie up her hands and take her to a wall room, put chain on her foot to prevent her running way, tie a rope round her waist and tie she to a column in the wall. Then later they loose the tie from the waist and tie her from one hand. In the same wall was seven other women, two dead a night after Dudie arrive and they carry them way. Jumbia say that Dudie tell them that they feed them on roast corn and water. On afternoons they would take them out to the sea and make them wash their skin. Ma Dudie bawl until she almost could not ketch she self, when she relate her ordeal to Massa Billinghurst. She tell the massa that one night one of the gal hold on to a man that come for her and she fast her teeth in he jaw bone and drive her hand in his face. After that some men grab she and hang

12. They were over-joyed and happy.

she to a post and lick she up mercilessly and then she Dudie did not hear anymore groaning. She think that the woman gone. But that was not it. Them rape she! When they done with her, they tie she foot and hang she from she foot and gradually lower her head in the water near by. Sometime later they put her into a boat and took her away. All the women see what happen.

Lady Jumbia say that they give Ma Dudie a good barking over a nine day period to take off the curse of the men. They also boil lavender bush together with bitter mint and give her to drink. Inflamation bush and barricada was another mixture they gave her. They also make she swallow the seed of the barricada bush, to make her vomit. Dudie was happy to escape the death and horror that she come close to. She was back at her home making she clothes and playing her banjo again happily with her people.

In those days people look at rape as a very terrible thing. It was the belief that no more sweetness could remain in the gal after a rape. If the village people get to know that a gal get rape shame would-kill she. She would quietly move out of the village and if she get the chance, would sink the land.

The Villagers and Dudie friends don't know the right story. If they ever get it, they would say all Dudie sweetness gone and they would scorn her. And so Lady Jumbia would tell Freeman's Village neighbours, but not Ma Dudie neighbours.

What the Billinghurst tell the friends was that some of the massa run short of people to work in the house and they hold Ma Dudie to do the work and he went to get her.

Quite some years after, I begin to get the story piece by piece from the Goodwins and some of their friends. Sometimes when me hear them talk about how the soldiers use to rape people I use to wish to God that Lady Jumbia was still around. The only difference between what I hear them say and what Jumbia tell the village people about Ma Dudie was that the Goodwins and some of the other bakkra talk about some kind of investigation in the behaviour of the Dockyard soldiers on the insistance of the Billinghurst family.

Jumbia never tell the village people about that part. Some planters have it to say that the investigation help speed up the return of most of the soldiers back to England. Most planters were against the soldiers because they haven't one scrap of respect for nobody. They abuse and rape anybody they ketch. The Goodwins say there was no special place at the Dockyard where they would hang the women. They would torture and kill them any place once they resist the soldiers and the soldiers call that kind of death "skin-a-cat".

The Goodwins side of the story also was that twenty-two women were in captivity at the Dockyard at the time. Seven from Guadeloupe, five from Montserrat and the rest from Antigua. The big surprise was women were in captivity on top of Monks Hill also. I don't remember the number they find there. Monks Hill was referred to as a carib look out before the planters name it after Colonel Monk. At one time the English use it for the same purpose as the Caribs. They build a wall right round the hill and it was another English strong hold in the land. On top of Monks Hill, was a large ball with lights around it. It could rise up through a scarfold up to several feet in the air. People could stay far away and see the moving ball. It would go up at 6 and 7 in the morning and at 12 noon, then at 4 in the afternoon and the last movement of the day was at 6:O'clock in the evening. It was the best guide to set some people to work and to break them off from work. We could stay at Belview Estate in the middle of the island and see the ball go up and down. Some English Planters use to spend their after crop holiday in the Great House on Monks Hill. But while soldiers and planters have them glee on the hill, the gals parents and friends were in sorrow. The main place the soldiers use to hold the women captive was close to the Nelsons Dockyard. The soldiers put up trash huts for the women to stay after they hold them inside the Dockyard and on Monks Hill for a time.

The trash huts grow in number and people begin to refer to them as The English Harbour. The word harbour has nothing to do with the sea shore near it. It come about because of the harbouring of the gals in the trash huts to work as prisoners and provide comfort for the soldiers. At times when the argument on the women captivity at the Dockyard came up, my boss and friends would say with smiling faces "Hawksbill hunch break up the soldiers sweetness all of a sudden". At other times they would argue that if Billy was not the keeper of the Duddie daughters, not a thing would happen. But as for me, I think God moves in mysterious ways and cause the Pinny hunch to break up what was without doubt the bloodiest and most shameful woman captivity of the land up to now.

The Goodwins always brag about the growth, richness and gleeful things at Hawksbill in the early days. They also talk and say "Where there is fun there is fart". So they talk about the murder, disappearances, rape and beatings that went on. My boss hadn't the slightest idea that I was drinking the story word for word and learning it by heart.

7
THE NEW GOLDEN TEXT:
Moravian and Methodist condemned

My mother and her close family did not go to live in any village for any length of time before I was born. According to her, her grandmother help to put up the village they call Free Wilbour. That was not too far from Vernons Estate, where the family live at the time. My mother story was that her family make a brief stop over in the new village and then go back to live with their man friend at Vernons.

I often remember how my mother use to fret continuously over the discomfort of the nega house we use to live in at Jonas Estate when I was a little boy. In her discomfort and worry, she would always quarrel and say that it was the kind of man that her parents use to dawid[1], was the capital cause that keep the family living on the plantation for so long after slavery. She could not understand why they did not truck up estate life like so many other people in the early years after the freedom. She was always on her bible

1. To be in love with.

oath[2] that their man friend was the real cause for the family to be on the plantation for that length of time. Her generation life style then, was to live down with man wherever they carry them.

A whole lot of the men use to love estate life, just to get to do woman as they like. And believe me, nothing trouble most men easily while they can comfort themselves with a woman.

Estate life, following the early years of the freedom, was an entirely different affair to the period when my mother was growing up. The bakkra that was my boss use to laugh when they hear some of the reasons my mother would give why her family remain on the plantation. Following a man friend could be one of the reasons good old George Goodwin would say. But in those days the massas use to allow so much laxity with the hope to prevent the ex-slaves from leaving the estates that they could elect freely not to leave. Maybe to stay was to them a better choice. The Goodwins also argue that after a time, the number leaving the estates was growing so much out of control, at one period, that many planters went out of their way to make life better for them. The massas would some-times shut them yie when they meet them eating butt[3] or interfering with anything to eat. They would also sweeten them up with pota-to or yam or other ground provisions that the massa would throw way. At other times they would give some left-over food. Except for the heart, the light and kidneys, the massas did not particularly eat any other part of the inside of animals and they would give the guts to their chosen. In those days, they also seldom eat the foot of animals either, and that too would be given away as part of the bait. Another reason the Goodwins suggested could be the cause for my mother and family to remain on the plantation was that the family got caught up on the plantation when things change for the worse with the village people and they could not leave even if they wanted to.

With all the sweetening up even at that time, no form of estate life was better than the New Village life. When the bakkra get

2. To swear.
3. A piece of sugar cane between the joints.

people not to leave them, most of the time, it was not more money or better privilege that they get. It was just some sweet mouth that fool them off. Massa just laugh up with some a them and that was enough. Up to now, some people think that they get more money when bakkra laugh with them or talk with them. My mother always want to get off the estate and she fight hard, hard to move away from it.

What the planters say concerning the reason why some people would elect to stay on the estates always worry me head. Whenever that argument come up, I try to make it go into one ear and fly through the next. I would be feeling good and proud if all my generation could boast like Lady Jumbia who lead gang after gang to set up shelter for people.

If I did have more sense when I was a boy growing up, I would surely learn more from Lady Jumbia. I was not the biggest person around then, but I learn quite a lot from her. The real truth is, I only know how valuable she was after she was dead and gone. I use to feel good when some bakkra say over so many things that she use to tell the village.

She told us of a constant war between the new village people and all the planters in the land. The bakkra was mortally against the setting up of the free villages. That was the root of the problem.

It was difficult for any priest or parson to sing sweet enough to get the majority of them to work for a slave massa again. The free village people make up their minds to make out with what little they could get until them dead. Whatever the hard time they have to face, before that time come, could in no way measure up to the rough time under the slave massas. After they begin to feel the freedom breeze they had no intention to let it pass by without using it up to the proper.

R.S.D. Goodwin talk about how the ex-slaves were lazy and did not like to work. He refer to them as the laziest generation of Antiguans on record. He use to complain that too may of them take the freedom to mean laziness and callousness. Many times he usually end his argument by saying, "I am not a god and I can never say that nobody at all, from what people call the free village, ever return by their free will to work on the estates, but that would be damn few. Damn few Sammy!" He use to tell me that the free people from Warner Estate would have music night after night in Free Warner. Who did not have music, would go by themself and drink grog. They set up as late as they want because they shub their own door. In fact, some would sleep a day time and drink their grog and make music in the night.

In slavery, smoking and drinking in the presence of the massas, was an unforgivable crime. Never happen! Slaves never even use to dream bout that. But the free people were drinking and smoking at will. Let me tell you , if the massas would get within close distance after the people feel the freedom, some would puff the smoke right into their faces. It would take nothing for the people of Free Warner to do more than that. It was freedom time on or off the plantation.

Lady Jumbia would say again and again "think of anything that a mortal should have liberty to do, the massas would stop them from doing it in slavery". I remember how she use to say if slavery did have little further to go, she think that her bones would be white long time[4]. She could not keep in anything, she would tell the neighbours. She have to show a sour face when subbon trouble her. And she would get her bottom cut to every cum-up[5] from massa. And her mother would slap she up for her to put her face good too. Massa vex, mother vex too. A slave could not openly show signs of disgust or displeasure. Very few slave massas, if you could find any at all, that would allow any sour face on the plantation.

Whatever the displeasure, the slaves would have to show a good face or run the risk of getting some good blows or no food for the day. When massa have to share licks on someone for having a sour face, he would say while giving them the blows, "You face long for nutton, me will mek um long for subbon".

4. She would be dead long ago.
5. She would be punished every time.

97

The slave massas in the land did not allow any slave to sing or hum in their hearing. They take the humming or singing to mean that the slave a banter them. Some bakkra ear light and would pick up the slightest singing or humming and some was mortally suspicious and would punish the innocent. According to Lady Jumbia, sometimes the massa don't hear a sound, but still throw his passion on them and lick them and would say at the same time - "Who de hell tell you I want to hear any singing round me". And the worse was to whistle. Nothing less than the cat-o-nine for that.

To put the hand on the jaw was another offence. The massa always shout down the slave with bad words for doing that. Massa always want to know what the dickance the slaves could be thinking bout to have the jaw in hand. That slave would have to explain why. Many times the slave would just beg him pardon. But massa may never want to hear anything bout pardon. Back then, Lady Jumbia use to mourn to us as if the ill treatment of slavery was still happening to her. The old lady would cry long water out she yie when telling us of the many slap she use to get in her face. She use to say that she would keep her hand at her jaw again and again without even knowing that her hand was at her jaw. Sometimes the slap come when she was not looking. At other times, the massa would rebuke her and then slap her. The slap give her headaches and pains in the neck and face. Slapping the slaves in the face was a regular punishment for that offence. Massa also wring their ears or pinch them up. The other punishment for putting the hand on the jaw was licks or missing a meal or not allowed any rest for the day. When others sit down to eat, little or big slave would have to jaunt up and down the field.

In slavery, there were many things that the slaves would do with the hope that massa would suffer. The massas have not the slightest clue bout them. If one was sitting and swinging the foot, massa would accuse that slave of swinging away her ma. But swinging the foot was to swing away the very massa. The slaves swing the foot with a wish that the massa would die. Another one was, cleaning the prongs of the fork with the handle of the fork resting on the ground, in the presence of the massa or when he had just turned his back, but not yet out of sight. That was also a wish of death to massa. By doing that, the slave was hoping that he would soon use the very fork to dig massa grave. To spit with vengeance, at the massa, was to wish him bad luck, distress, suffering and death. Send him on his way! What Lady Jumbia say was that the slaves had to be smart when doing this one. That was done when massa was sighted from a distance or his back was away from the slave who was carrying out the wish. To spit at a person, back then, was deemed a horrible thing. The slaves, when doing this, would fire out the spit with a loud sound...pem...pem...pem. They did not just spit and allow the normal sound to come out of the mouth - the person would make the sound, with a vengeance.

Sometime in the 1830's, a slave from Warner Estate was beaten to death because he hark and spit plumb in the face of one massa Benn. That happen when the slaves gather at the estate for orders one morning. Before he do that he would have already pre-dicted that it would be the lass-a-he[6]. The biggest thing was the deliberate humiliation he left with massa Benn. He could not take it. He had to run away. Shame! Could not face a soul - neither slave nor his own kind. He left the land with speed. Slave spit in-a bakkra face? You would not even understand what that mean. Anyone of them bakkra that happen to, would surely have to clear-out. Could never stick round. According to Lady Jumbia, things that the ex-slaves use to do in secret before the freedom, they begin to do openly. Not looking back for a soul! The Antiguan old slave massas could not believe what they were seeing and hearing.

Some of them who never dream that the ex-slaves could even see a school door or even go to church, change their minds. According to the Goodwins, the planters talk their minds to the Govenor again and again. They tell him that something must be done to bring the ex-slaves back in line. They also talk hard to the

6. It almost goes without saying that for any slave to spit in the face of a massa, the punishment would be death.

church big people because the parsons and priest were not doing their duty to the Queen's subjects. They must find a way to curb the reckless behaviour of the people they set free or all the good planters will have to leave the land and it will surely become bankrupt and another nation would take it.

At last a group of planters ask the Mother Country to call on the churchmen to work out a formula of learning that will change the ways of the ex-slaves and to let them abide by what is for the good of the colony. The Governor at the time call a meeting with the top church people. Among the people at the meeting were the Methodists, Moravians and Church people for the Mother Country. They all come to a decision to use a part of the church building in the land for school. The church would select the teachers and the Governor would pay them. The day school was to be on two days a week; Mondays and Wednesdays. The teachers would also take classes on Sundays at Sunday School.

Mark you, understand me quite well. All the noise the Planters make about slave behaviour, they never have in mind that the churchmen would come up with the idea of a day school or any school for nega people. I believe, the formula of learning the planters had in mind was to do subbon for the ex-slaves to go be-order[7]. My mother tell me that some semblance of public school start in the 1850's and the school day was every Wednesday.

The day school was mostly in the afternoon - The morning hours was to do anything they were call upon to do. The Moravian and Methodist was doing all they could with their own day school long time.

Sometimes in life one contention is not done before the other start. This time the Moravian and Methodist parsons enter into some serious quarrel with the planters and the Anglican priests. This quarrel was bitter, bitter. Nearly ketch to fight! Sometimes when the older heads tell this tory, I think I see them in their gown heated and ready to throw blows at one another. Those priests use

7. The intent of the planters was to devise a formula of learning, that will condition the ex-slave, to be obedient and do as told.

to love to hit nega people. My mother say that the bitterness come just because the Moravians find out that when the ex-slaves go to buy at the shops, the shopkeepers was robbing them blind. Because of this, the Moravians start to make noise all over the land about it. That was from the pulpit to open-air services to the door steps. They ask the people to come to Sunday school, so that they could teach them the Word of the Lard and also how to count their money. This swell the Moravian Sunday School and the Church following. The Methodist follow-suit. The Methodists would certainly loose members if they did not join in and do the same thing.

In those days, the Methodist and the Moravian were always jealous against each other. The Anglican was against the two of them. Stiff competiton was always the case between the Methodist and the Moravian. Anything one do, the other was sure to do.

And so both of them take on the task to teach the poor people how to count money. Some ex-slaves would know that a shilling is more than a sixpence but could not say by how much. Most of them just did not know how much change they should get back when they go to buy goods. So too they did know if they have enough money to buy the goods. The business people in the land, at that time, were all former slave massas. They take it to make a habit to rob the ex-slaves of their money when they go to buy their goods. The Goodwins tell me that the business poeple use to have some hearty laugh at the free people when they did not understand that they were robbing them blind. The ex-slaves would tell them thanks. They would also say to them, "God bless you, massa" or "God bless you, misses". The people were not anyway close to be able to relate the value of money against goods or labour. How to count the money was on the mind of everybody. At Sunday School, the Moravian put in their heads that everyone must tell the parson what they want to buy and parson will say how much pennies to carry and parson will tell them where to shop. Parson tell them to shop at one place, that will make parson know the robber quicker.

There was hardly a bakkra in this land that was not mad, mad with the Moravians and the Methodists. They accuse them of playing with hell fire that will surely get out of control and that they were digging their own graves to be teaching ex-slaves how to count money.

Lady Jumbia tell the neighbours that the planters call a meeting with the leaders of the Methodist and the Moravian to point out the folly of their ways and ask them to stop putting certain things in the head of the ex-slaves. The Anglicans tell them that kind of teaching was out of place, and was not the business of the Church. Uncontrollable dangers are sure to come if they continue to open the ex-slaves yie like that. Make them learn the counting themself. If they continue, it will back fire on Moravian, Methodist, Anglicans everybody. The Moravian and the Methodist people won't be said. They just won't be said[8]. At the Sunday school they would show them the different money and teach them how to count. In the week, sometimes, they would have a mock sale to test them.

I hardly think that it was ever made clear to us that a slave would have to be real good and lucky to see and hold any kind of money when in bondage. That never happen in this land. Enough praise have not been given, first to the Moravian and then to the Wesleyan preachers, for their braveness to begin to teach poor people how to count money, at that time, and against such kind of fury.

In fact, I don't remember hearing anyone talking about it, since Thaddeus James, Freeman's Village, Methodist local preacher, dead. That gone and forgotten, long time! The older people of Freeman's Village use to send collection to the church even though they did not go to the service. That was the recompense. The older heads did not forget to say thanks.

According to Lady Jumbia, in order for the Sunday School to be able to do the teaching of knowing the money, the Methodist of Freeman's Village, make three groups, one for pickenega, another one for the big size people. When I say big size people I mean those that will soon go to work. The other part, was for them that

8. Won't budge, standing firm to their actions and beliefs.

was working already. Those that happen to take in the teaching a little, use to boast how they can count their own money. Lady Jumbia always praise the Freeman's Village Methodist Church Sunday School. She tell the neighbours that it was there she learn to count money a little and to spell her name and know it. She also use to say that she took a long time before she could write it. She would take a bit of stick and print her name on the earth, not on paper, as people would think now. And she would say the older people take the longest to take in the learning. She use to tell the neighbours too, that the great wish of the people after they come to their senses, was to be able to know money, learn[9] to talk, learn to spell their name and know it when them see it. And the biggest one was to know some verses from the Bible and Hymn book and to be able to say them over or sing them. It was the feeling then that the best way to be able to get to talk good was to memorize things and say them over and over. That was also the quickest way to get recognition. To get to do this, Sunday School was the place. And so the Moravian and the Methodist take the time to make sure that the poor ex-slaves learn the new Golden Text that is nowhere in the bible. At that time, the Sunday School Golden Text, become the most talk about thing in the land. There was the all out race to see who could memorize the Golden Text and repeat it to the end. Some people did not go to Sunday School to hear anything else but how to count money. Rag up and dirty would be there. After a time some people that don't know a ting could count money more than some of them who know a little hymn or two.

My mother say at Gilbert Sunday School the parson larn them[10] that sixpence bigger than the bit and the bit, bigger than tree-copper, and the tree-copper bigger than the half-o-bit. And that two hapenny[11] come one penny; two penny come to half-o-bit and a penny is a copper. And after they take in that, my mother say they learn them, that a copper worth a goods from three coppper, left

9. Learn.
10. Teach them.
11. Half penny.

half-o-bit in hand. Three copper from bit and a half, left three copper in hand. The bit and a half is the sixpence. That is what the Methodist at Gilbert teach my mother and she teach all she picknee the same thing. That was the new Golden Text[12]. Mark you, that Golden Text was not found in the Bible. But it is the Golden Text that taught our people how to count money. It is our people Golden Text that cause the wrath of the Anglican planters to decend visciously on the Moravian and Methodist and me Papa Sammy call it the unforgetable Golden Text.

Bit-and-a-half   One Bit   Three Copper   Half-a-Bit

A Copper   A Copper

Hapney   Hapney

Some of the money used in earlier times

12. A verse or passage one memorizes from the Bible.

8

CULTURE BLOOMS:
Masses yearn for school

Black people in this land way of life change drastically after slavery, and woman and man start to take pride in themself. The woman was more keen than the man in beautifyng-up themself. They pay special attention to the head. Black women seldom wear dress hats. Dress hat belongs to the bakkra misses[1]. The custom back then was that a woman would cover her head while she was under a roof. That was a mark of respect. Black women use to wear the henkitra[2] on their head. At one stage, nothing else was there for them to wear on the head, and they would tie the henkitra in all manner of styles.

According to my mother almost every headtie style had a meaning. There was the headtie style that mean that a gal was free, single and have not a man to keep her back, but at the same time she was looking for a fella. The headtie they use to banter the looser in a love war was a big one. That's the one that tell people that she win out the love fight between herself and another woman for a

1. The wife of the white plantation owner.
2. A piece of cloth that was wrapped around the head in various styles.

man. I don't think that this generation or even the one that just past ever hear of the Ratreal Head tie. Thats the tie that mean that the woman have enough picknee and that she done from all man. She say time up. It would take a brave man to see that headtie and still ask the woman question.[3]

Back then too, when a woman just confine, she would wear the headtie to let out the secret and man would know that she is tender. Also too, there was the special headtie that the woman healers use on sick people. The tie was slack enough to let enough air to the head and at the same time hold in the bush under and above the headtie.

The headtie fashion that was very common is the one the young gal use to wear to meet a sweetheart. This fashion was use when them gals was in for a spree. At some point she may clash with other gals over a man. When this happens woman tie the henkitra around the waist as a sign that they would colar any man or woman to win the love battle.

The woman that use to teach the Sunday school wore a different head tie. So too was the woman that teach the day school.

I see quite a lot of women wearing plenty of the old headtie styles. I am not sure if any one of them have a clue of the reason for them. The only one that I don't see at all is the one that the bakkra misses use to put on them young gal picknee when they want people to believe that them a maid. Back then when some bakkra misses want the son of a rich bakkra to notice their daughter they would make sure that she wear that headtie. Sometimes they would wear a hat with the headtie.

The same way the women them use to have the many different headtie fashion was the same way they would sport with different hair styles. To say what they have in their stomach with the headtie or the plait hair without opening the mouth was a way of life then. In those days young people could not talk any man and

3. In the case to make sexual advances.

woman torry in the hearing of big people. Make no mistake, they would get blow. Sometimes a stick cross the head or where ever they get it. Not like now a days when picknega and big people big a like. Young people use to have to hide secretly to carry on any man and woman argument. That was one of the reasons why they plan how to talk with mouth shut. Plus, not many things were there to do and out of that lifestyle come the many customs and the many sayings that seem so funny today.

The women back then use to take extra special care of the hair. I think that the two main wish of the young gal in those days was to have long hair and to have picknee. A woman hair was regarded as her beauty. They would wash the hair with the kind of plant they know would grow the hair long, as long as they could get them.

People do different kinds of things to make the hair grow long. The wild ochro was a precious thing for that purpose. So too was the sinkle-bible, the cassie and the cactus. People also call the cactus dull-dull. This is not to be mistaken with the dull-dull that the women use for painful monthly things. People also cook the cactus in fungi; a good substitute for ochro. Every thing don't agree with everybody the same way, but to me wild ochro was the most capital thing for the growing of the hair. Hot the water to boiling point, put in the wild ochro or the cassie, which ever you have, allow the water to cool off then wash the head. Try it. I don't think that any shampoo or whatever they call the thing they use today to wash the hair can be better. The old natural way make the head feel cool and the hair grow longer. Nega people hair grow long when they comb and plait them regularly. No water needed for the dull-dull - neither hot nor cold.

Pick off the cassie, crush it up in a thin cloth like a net and rub it in the head. This will prevent the fibre from sticking up in the hair when it dry out. The coconut was also for hair growing. Grate the coconut and ring the juice in the head, plait and tie it up. The coconut oil for the greasing of the hair and skin is also capital. In those days man use to despise a picky head woman. Some would have a picky head woman in the same bracket as a barren woman. The long hair was the thing. A beautiful woman was one that have nuff-tun-a-hair on her head. The present generation may not understand me when I say the measurement use at that time to put a woman in the beauty box, was the length of her hair. A woman could be beautiful with hair long for-so, but she can't bring picknee. The man would left she or don't have much to do with her. Bringing the picknee come first. The man would look for the woman that have the two things, hair and can breed. I think that barren woman in those days were far and few between. People use to say a god cuss on the woman that is barren and that a picky head woman was one that people think was saddled with endless days of grief. Back then, a woman, when she chimb off her hair was telling of deep sorrow or loss. When a woman clean her hair off her head, it was to tell people that there was a death of a beloved family member. When some one did not care over something, they would use the phrase - "That won't mek me chimb off me head", or they would say, "me can't pwoil me beauty for that."

There was the hair style that mean that the woman done with all man. Another hair style would show that a woman win out the love fight between she and the other woman. She would plait from back of the head to the centre and from the front to the centre. She would tie both ends together with a red cloth or place a red rose in the centre facing the front. And in this land there was the popular one that mean that the woman have plenty mouth to feed, plenty picknee without owner. There was the one where the young gal was telling everybody that she have she fella a ready. There was also the one that was telling people that this gal has a new lover and nobody can go wid she. She is on top of the world is how the people would put it now.

In days way back then, people use to have a way to name things, mostly trees. Every name had a meaning. I can't count the many different croton flower trees. The people in days gone by had aname for everyone of them. I know very well the one the people use to call "Me Want-You Na Want" and also, the one they call "Have And To Hold". The "Home Sweet Home" Croton Tree is very much around and so too is the one that carry the name "Lea-Me-Lone".

When a woman left a man and another woman hold on to the same man with speed that woman would plait the hair in a circle, and stick in the hair a leaf of the Croton flowers that they call "Me Want-You Na Want". She would banter the other woman and show off with the man. The woman that live with a man and want to make people believe that she is very happy and comfortable would stick a leaf of the "Have And To Hold" croton in she hair. She would carry the "Lea-Me-Lone" croton flowers when she and her lover have falling out.

The women mostly plait the hair to resemble the rope, and rows in the sugar cane fields. As you know, sugar and plough land was the go then. When they plait the hair evenly backwards and tie all the ends together with cloth or ribbon, the colour would spell out the state of mind. White mean wanting no interference from any man. Let the peace dwell. Black would indicate she is on the spree with her lover or she is happy. Red would mean that she could take on any man.

The hair and headtie styles that have to do with love affair, was the most plentiful at singing meetings and tea meetings and at festive times. It was the same thing at the Put-Me-Up and Put-Me-Down concert. The Moravians start that kind of concert sometime at the end of the 1850's. That concert got the name because someone in the audience would pay for some one to sing, or laugh, or cry or recite. Pay to do anything. It was a concert with plenty of laugh. At the same time, another person would pay to put the person down off the stage, or to stop the singing, or laughing or what they pay them to do. Sometimes they would put up two people that are not talking together to dance with each other. When a gal will not talk to a man that a ded for she[4], that man would quietly get someone to

4. To be deeply in love with a person without the person's knowledge.

pay to put them up to dance - plenty of fun was in that. My mother use to say that the Methodist and the Moravian put-she-up to sing or to do the easy up and easy down hop, and she could not do anything about it. She also use to tell the neighbours that the put-me-up and put-me-down concert keep some people heart together and help them leave their problem home because they get plenty laugh. Whether the gal was going to a singing meeting or tea meeting or to church, or to a put-me-up and put-me-down concert, the gals use to dress good. Man and woman in this land love plenty cloth long time. That is the thing up to now - But it was barefoot time. Not a shoes. A few people who happen to have shoes would tie the strings together and throw them across the shoulders until they reach the service or programme where they would put them on. After the programme, back over the shoulders, the shoes would go until they reach home. A pair of shoes would serve from one picknee to the next and the next. Back then, women dress fit them well pass the knee. Normally they make them with a band on the waist or a band would be at each side of the dress and both bands would tie together in a bow at the back. The sleeves would drop on the elbow and the upper part would cover the collar bone right up to the neck. The dress would have a slit in the back to enable it to pass over the head. Buttons or pins or cloth sewn on each side was the thing to close up the back. It was not too long after slavery, before the people in the villages have someone, that make clothes that could fit right. Old George Goodwin, one time big planter of Antigua and owner of Gaynors Estate, use to say that he have to respect the ex-slaves for how they learn to make clothes so quick and so good. But my mother say that making clothes good did not come all that easy. The people that use to count themself the biggest in the land after the Planter and the Priest in slavery days was them that make clothes.

Before the freedom, clothes making was a tight, tight secret for a long time. The slaves that learn the trade were those that work in the buff under the tight control of massa. They were the slowest to leave the plantation.

Some were so well fasten to the buff that up to the time the freedom come they take long to understand that the chain was off their foot. The argument was that some of them go on as if they did not want it off. The bakkra friends refuse to make clothes for the free people who leave the plantation but the free people cut and contrive.

In a while, they were good at making shirt, waist coat, frock and pin-a-fore but did not get into the nock of making trousers and jackets that readily. The collar also was hard to make and most shirts and jackets were without collar.

People would cut down trees that have trunks and branches that shape like human waist with two legs and use them as guage when making trousis. The tailor would measure out of his head what he think was the rightful size of the person, and then base up on the trousis tree. There was difficulty getting the right length of the crotch. The waist was, at most times bigger than that of the person. Whatever the type of clothes the people make, was usually cut bigger than the actual fit so they would not run the risk of spoiling the cloth. Too big was always a fit. That was a popular phrase then. Almost all the men and boys use to wear bracers made of cloth, and tack on to the trousers back and front. Later they make them to use with button. No belt or string around the waist for pickee nega. It was the saying that it retard their growth. Trousers pockets was attach on the outside. A trousers then had at most two pockets, one in front and the other behind on the side of the hand the person use most. After a time, anybody would find it difficult to find a single village without a tailor that make man clothes and a seamstress making woman clothes. In those days, man fancy the double breasted jacket. That take the longest to conquer. So too, they use to have a big dolly tuff with grass for the guage of the clothes for the upper part of the body. There was no tape measure, no rule, nothing to measure any soul. The dolly usually have shoulder length down to the elbow. Little by little the people get to master the clothes making.

Big stumbling block stand in the way of everyday life back then. When it comes to the book work, reading, writing, spelling and how to talk - a mean how to call words right, the people could not move on one bit. That was a big problem. That was a big big spoke in a arwe wheel.[5] Somebody must teach them. They could not move on in this direction without getting help. The Methodists and Moravians were doing a little thing at the Sunday School.

Mark you, the Sunday school could not cater for the education of the whole population. A great many of the people that do a little teaching at the Sunday School, could not call words properly. They could not tell when a word was put in the wrong place. The argument of the planters was that there was no money to pay teachers to get day school going. The lack of schooling prevent the people from learning to call words properly and also cause them not to have good speech for long, long years.

The Moravians that use to have the rush for the Sunday School did not have many teachers who could talk good English.[6] The Goodwin family of Collins Estate use to say that English was not the mother tongue of the early Moravian preachers that come here at the time and that God knows that most people could not understand them readily. The Methodist was different. Their preachers come from the Mother Country but only one or two would be around at that time. Another poblem was, the Bakkra in Antigua who could help, had very little to do with both the Methodist and the Moravian and that means the poor people.

As tiny as this land is, almost every group of people on the different plantation use to have a different slant in the tongue. That surely tell me how tight the control on the movement of the slaves was.

Part of the work I use to do was to barter and buy animals for the estates that belong to the Goodwin family. I was their all in

5. It is obvious that educating the post slave generations was not one of the primary goals of the planter class.
6. It was assumed that, speaking like the English planters was considered good English.

all, but was very special on this subject. Sometimes their friends would borrow me to do that business for them. They would depend on me heavily for proper advise before they do any business of the kind. I can't remember them doing that kind of business without me, between 1900 and up to the time when all of them dead out.

This business bring me in contact with many different people and even though all of us do the bad talking, some places were bad, bad, bad. A hardly could understand some of them when I meet them first. At one time I was under the impression that the people hardest to understand was the people from Willikies and the surrounding area in the far east. Then when I start to travel in the Cedar Grove area it take me long to understand them too. The problem was even worst in the south side from the estate of Bolans right through Crabb Hill, Johnsons Point and Urlings. Although Jennings and Old Road are in that area, the people there use to talk much differently to the other parts of the South.

The people that live in and around the Willikies Compound and near it would begin the opening of their sentence with words like daay-daay. They would use it as if they were surprise over something. They would say daay ee a come. Meaning the person is coming. They also would say daay ee ya. Meaning the person is here. They would say daay a trouble now: Meaning the person get into trouble. They would also say daay ee wok. Meaning the person work hard. They would use certain phrases that I could not follow like, daa-wan-do-dey or draw-ee-day, and the tongue would roll fast, fast sometimes.

The North side which include Cedar Grove Estate use to love to use the word -um-a. They would say um a come. Meaning the peson is coming. A woman would say -um man hax me fu lub. Meaning the man want to make love with her. Cedar Grove was the um estate. They use to use um-a for the start of every expression, um-ya, um-ya tief, um-ded-ded or phrases like draw-um-dey um-ya-dey.

In the Southern side, the people would call the word, sumart

- for smart, sumit for Smith or sumall for small. They would start their expression with ee and daay bo - ee man goo-on wok - ee man dies; ee too tief. Daay, bo come ya. Meaning boy come here. They use to say hopen for open. The people in the south also use the word hax. It was easy to say no hax me nutton, meaning don't ask me nothing. They would say me see-so. Meaning I say so. Dee man hib me dung. That is to say the man throw me down. For the word because, some estate people would use the word becausing, others say becausen and quite a few still say becausa.

The people in the whole land use to use all kinds of words. Our past generation make their own words. The people use to like to add or take off the letter "S". It was common to hear people use the words - they says - they comes - they becomes, keem for scheme, tory for story and trang for strong, pwoil for spoil. It was common to hear them say not noor, meaning they do not know. Today young people who know better laugh heartily and some times mock the older heads when we talk the old way. They would skin-up their faces when they hear com ya, or go dey, or come ya-so-so, but that's how the people know it then - It was a long, long road getting to know better.

Plenty names change because the people use to have problems calling them. If the names was long, they would drop off piece either from the end or the beginning. A time ago there was a lot of people in this land that carry the title St. John. Our people take off the St. and just say John. So too there was plenty people with the name Robertson and the people just drop off the son and say Roberts. There was Gregory and we change it to Greg and so it was. One day somebody may make a list of the lost names. For years and years running up to right now, most nega people register two names at birth that have nothing to do with the title. The second name become the title because there was no father.

Twisting words or phases was all too common. We use to answer yea instead of yes. The bakkra never call the nega man Mister or women Mistress. They use to call the men Bo, Bo Sammy or Bo Kenneth. The women they would say See Mary or See Kate, or Ma Mary or Ma Kate. Mothers follow the bakkra and call their man picknee Bo. They would say wa-do-you-Bo, Bo-Bo- or com ya Bo. Bo-Bo wa do you. And for the gal, they call her See or Ma. Come Ma. Come see - Come see see. That was later changed to Sis-Sis. Later one of the sis get drop off and now they say come Sis. For the word Mother - we use to say Mooma. For the word man nearly all my generation say mon. Potikiller we say for particular and so it was.

All of us talk bad until some get to improve on it bit by bit. Except for some big shot people that live in the town, only the generation of the 1960's show some difference in the talking since I was born. That is because of the school now, the teaching and the people trying to talk better. On a number of times, the planters I work with would say to me "Sammy how you talk so good and the others round the place talk so bad?" The bakkra also have beams to understand the people too. The only thing I know is that I listen to the bakkra keenly and learn some words. I have been in their close company for a long long period and me pick up a word or two, but I don't know for sure when I talk what they call the correct English. Even the word eye, I would hardly say it. I would say yie more often.

Many times when me talk some of my grand children would tell me that I am not using the right English. Another time they would say I am mixing up the past tense with the present and the future. They would laugh and tell me how I should say it. At other times they would say me sound good. Then all of a sudden they would say the old man a pluck up the grammar tree. Not a thing me know bout good grammar and those things. I never hear bout them when I was young. Me can't deliberately put them how they should go or match them up. This old man don't know head nor tail of what they mean by past, present and future tense.

I don't know when I am making a mistake or when I should not use words that would cause the young people to open their mouth wide. To them I call words out of tune many times and at other times they would say me sound good - me a speak. Too often when me talk they would smile or laugh when I don't fit the words properly as they know them today. I can spell and understand much more than I can talk what people call good english. Almost all the nega people in this land that born before or a little after me can't talk at will what people call the good grammar or the good english. All me know this old man try to talk just for people to understand me. While they understand, that's it. People like me cannot knock up with the thing they call the grammar. Now-a-days I don't think that I ever talk a minute and don't use the good english, the broken grammar and all the things they call the tense at the same time wrongfully. At other times when I place the words right that would be purely by accident. I don't think if my generation did go to school there would be this big problem with the calling of words. I don't feel no way when this generation laugh because of how I place me words sometimes. From my experience the forming of the tongue, take long, long to come by and the bad talking is not going to stop in a hurry.

Now-a-days, the normal picknee talk at age two or three. In my day, the same picknee take up to six, seven years to begin to call words for people to understand. Sometimes they would reach small gang[7] and can't talk for anybody to understand them. In those days, mothers did not even know that they should teach the picknee how to talk. Little children was left to do almost everything by themselves. The most they do was to cry for food and when they cry, they would say ma-ma or pa-pa or da-da. Quite often those words become the name they call their mother. Pickenega start to call their mother mommy or modder and the father daddy in the 1930's. That was after people begin to learn new words. Tongue can't tell how life have become different today. Back then, never mind how the singing sound sweet, one would certainly understand the tune, but however keen they listen, they could never hear the words. People

7. A form of child labour used on the estates during and after slavery.

could not get the words to put them properly. The majority of Antiguans love them singing and they would let the sound come through the nose. Even those that can't turn tune would sing out loud. Woman would la-la or sing a tee-la-lum or a tee-la-la or a bamba-bambaya-bambaya repeating them again and again. They would hum and hum and then break into a tee-la-la or so again. The man would sing the latest bena. It was the regular thing for a man to sing -O-Bamba-lay-woman-go-kill-me, Oh-Bamba-lay-hungry go kill me or Work go kill me.

At one time I use to believe that all the people that belong to the Mother Country talk the same. In my early life I did not have the opportunity to meet people from the surrounding islands. The mixing of people from the islands start to pick up near the end of the century. That was the time when Antigua become head of the Leeward Islands and policeman start to go constantly to and fro. The real mixing pick up steam sometime after the beginning of the twentieth century. From the mixing, our people could tell just by the way the person talk which island that person come from. Whether from St. Kitts, Montserrat, Barbuda or which one of them. I find Antiguan accent was no way close to any of the nearby islands. That baffle me. I never had in mind that the tongues would be so different. When I begin to meet Barbudans regularly, that even shock me more because the Barbudan tongue is so far away from the Antiguan tongue. I could not believe it. To be perfectly fair though, I think that the Barbudan tongue was closer to the people of Johnson's Point and Urlings in the south, than to the rest of the island.

As time pass I get to know from planters that work in Jamaica and others that meet Jamaicans, that the Antiguan tongue was close to the Jamaican tongue. This use to marvel me, because from what I hear, Jamaica is no way close to Antigua. And the island that close by talk so different to them from Antigua.

While people from the neighbouring islands go in and out of

Antigua, there was no known Jamaican family that use to live in this place. In fact, I know for sure I become old before I was able to meet a Jamaican or know of any in Antigua.

I would venture to say that most Antiguans then was like me. The first Jamaican I happen to see and hear was Marcus Garvey. The Black Starline leader that I always hear bout. I went to hear him at the Anglican School room in the mid 1930's. Believe me, when I hear the man, I open me mouth wide, wide, a couldn't believe it. The man talk close, close to the people that live in the south of Antigua. The Goodwins did not want me nor the people to go to hear Garvey. A whole lot of the planters become unhappy with the Anglican Bishop, because he rent Garvey the Cathedral School Room for the talk. It was tre-copper per person to enter. Garvey say the fee was to offset the cost of the building. The next morning early and bright I tell Boss Goodwin that I went to hear Marcus Garvey and that his tongue was like that of the people round south and what could be the reason for such a closeness when Jamaica was so far away from Antigua.

I remember very well R.S.D. Goodwin want to know first what Garvey have to tell the people before he answer me. My boss face become heavy. I tell him that Garvey talk of the many problems of race hatred and poverty that black people have to suffer at the hands of the white man in the whole world and that the black people should come together to save ourself. And that he tell the people that every blackman have the rope tie at the same place round his neck. Before R.S.D. Goodwin answer me, he murmur and say Antigua people don't need Garvey to take any rope from round them neck. The people here dam happy, too happy. My boss was vex and me think for a while that he was not going to answer me. However, after his face get back level he tell me that the connection he know bout Antigua and Jamaica was that the Nugent Family in Jamaica use to get slaves dog cheap from the Gold Coast and Dahome and they use to make regular shipment from Jamaica to the Nugent family in Antigua and the other way round for many years.

This Nugent family and their company use to engage in large scale exchange of slaves between Jamaica, Antigua and Haiti. He say they use to land them at Johnson's Point wharf. Many planters he said get slaves from the Nugent Family right up to the time when the trade stop. They use to hold them in the dungeon at the Johnson's Point wharf.

R.S.D. Goodwin as usual, always go out of his way to prove to me or anybody, bakkra or no bakkra that he know what he was about. And so he tell me that the man that hold the last set of slaves that come from Jamaica for the Nugent Family, was a bakkra they call K. Wall Sheridan. His family own Cades Bay Estate at the time, and the Nugent Slaves coming from Jamaica or wherever travel straight from one family to the other.

The other reason that Massa Goodwin claim that could cause the closeness in the tongue was the wide spread duncy-head-edness that take place in Antigua and Jamaica for years and years and get worse year after year. He also said that hardly anyone was in sight to guide or help develop the tongue of the ex-slaves proper-ly for quite some time after the freedom. The accent of the planters could also have something to do with the way the people talk.

I remember, R.S.D. Goodwin also say that some of the ships that bring the slaves from Jamaica to Antigua were the Elizabeth, Susana, Gally and the Greyhound Gally. Later that day he write the names on a piece of paper for me and I learn them be heart as many other things.

He also let me know that Jamaica suffer worse than all the other islands combine, because of many many years of starvation. That cause great suffering on the people and that Garvey was more needed in Jamaica than in Merica or in Antigua. R.S.D. Goodwin make sure that I hear him and so he go on and on against Garvey.

Before the argument done Frank join the conversation. As usual he support his brother. I surely let them know that Marcus Garvey talk well and proper and that I get a soft, soft spot in my heart for all Jamaicans after I hear him. I tell them that, I give the doorman an extra six-pence to help. I tell the Goodwin Brothers, that I have to get a queen conch shell for Garvey. That was how my heart go out for the man.

In days of old when the old poor people want to show their love to someone and they want to let them know that they deserve the highest honour of the land, they would present them with a queen conch shell.

The women in my young days, always say that the queen conch shell when given to anyone is a symbol of strength and a gut feeling that the person is sincere and would decide to meet any hard time and make sacrifice for the good of people.

I get to know from my mother that the women at Hawksbill Estate back then use to have the queen conch shell as the highest honour that they could give to anyone. The saying was when any-one give the queen conch shell to a person that person will remember the one who give the gift until death. It was also given to show everlasting love between a man and a woman.

I get a fisherman we call Lammy Leg from All Saints Village to get the queen conch shell for me. He stay long to get it. The only thing I do then was to send my pleasant thoughts for the man that I think was blessed.

I feel bad, bad when Garvey explain how his own race call upon the white man to jail him. I get the creeps when he tell the gathering how his own race crooked him and with that he could not escape humiliation. He believed if it was not for them he would not suffer work house and then deportation from Merica. He started to make the negro in Merica at least be better off. And I remember him saying that the blow scatter them. That they won't be able to have the real power nor get respect for many many years to come. The Garvey talk make me feel sorry for my own people. I always hope for the day to come when all of us will work to protect each other, I hope that the new and coming generation will check to find out the real reason for the closeness of the tongue between Antigua and Jamaica and to see if what Massa R.S.D. Goodwin say is the reason for the closeness.

All I know is that the many people I meet from the different islands with different tongues may have differences in the talking but we all have the same troubles and way of life.

Social, Cultural and Academic Disposition:
Pointing towards Monsterrat, Lady Jumbia explaines to a crowd of on-lookers that Nigeria (in Africa), her ancestral homeland, lies just west of the island of Monsterrat which is visible from the coast of Antigua. Monsterrat, she explains, blocks her eyes and theirs from seeing her beloved Nigeria.

The ruins of the village named after William Wilberforce. The local people called the village Free Wilber. Situated south of Parham on the hill between Parham and Parham Hill, it was one of the the earliest villages set up after slavery ended.

More than one hundred and sixty years after slavery ended, the Irish Hangman Stone still sits on Hawhsbill estate. This is perhaps the most famous stone in Antigua. It served as a platform for the gallows on which the English used to hang slaves and Irish people.

Hawksbill Rock is situated just some yards but in sea across from the estate. The estate got its name from the rock because the rock's shape is like a hawk's bill.

The ruin of hawksbill leap house, fun house and great house. A passage way used to join all three houses together on Hawksbill estate. The compound was used for housing massa and family, special functions and having fun time.

Known as the "trousis tree" in earlier times, tailors would use its trunk and branches as a yardstick or measuring tool when making trousis. Sometimes too the tailors would just have a guess on the rightful size. It is reversed for measurement

Hair styles like the one above was common in earlier times. This particular style means that "the woman had plenty mouths to feed." Each plait represented a child in the family. In this case, it would be thirteen.

Part old, part new of the famous Gilbert step when Methodism was born in the Americas and where Papa Sammy's mother attended school.

9
SUSTAINING LIFE:
Wonder of Countless
Ages

One of the big-big things that the people take on after the freedom, was that they live with the mind that they must know as much as possible about the bush and the plants. All have a use. They live with the belief that to know about them, was to know about life itself. How to lessen pain. What to use to prolong life with some measure of comfort. What each kind of bush was good for. How to use them. People back then would do everything to make sure that they were always in a position to come up with the right answer. The exact dose of the bush water. What bush to put on the body. What bush was good for what. That was a very important thing. There was the crave to know more about them all the time.

In those days, the people in the south of the island and in particular the village of Old Road, use to know about the bush and the plant remedy more than other places. In places like Warner and

Bendals in the mid south, they too would know a lot. Don't be mistaken! There were many good woman healers all over the land. There was not a village that did not have their own. It was just the case that the very best could be found at Old Road for long, long years. Everybody always have a favourite. Some people will choose Liberta as the place to find the best healer. Others would favour Folly Hill or Swetes or Buckleys. That is how life go. But generally speaking, the majority of the people in the land believe Old Road healers have the edge.

People from all parts of the land use to travel to the southern villages to get to know as many kind of bush and plant as they could. It was a rare thing to find something growing in the other parts of the land that did not grow in certain parts in the south. That part get more rain. The reason for a more fertile place. The knowledge of what the bush or plant is good for come from many years of experience and teaching. Some slaves would also bring the knowledge with them.

Slaves were not all that fooly.[1] It was the bondage that kill them knowledge and experience and the pressure finally turn most a them fooly. They would certainly have the attitude of "way ee drop ee tap".[2] No knocking up.[3] This would be for most people when in bondage.

I cannot tell a soul how it actually begin to happen, but it was the real truth that the people of Old Road was the first to start to spread the knowledge about the bush remedy I know of none who say differently. Woman healers use to go to Old Road to take lesson bout bush remedy and to keep up to date on new found out. There was some popular names from that village that the people use to hear all over this land. Names like Ma Juky, Lady Scott, Mama Countis and Ma Cilma. How good them be. Who better than who. Who have the rush. People use to say that they never miss. Call any

1. Foolish.
2. To be content with anything.
3. To make no effort for change they were in a state of helplessness.

bush or plant. They could tell what it was good for. Sometimes they give the bush or tree the name they think that they should call it. And the magic that I cannot explain is that these women healers, at that time, could not say the very first letters in the A,B,C.

My mother use to follow my grandmother and other people again and again to Old Road when she was a growing up young gal to learn and know the remedy. My family was living at Vernons Estate then. On foot was far and tiresome from Vernons to Old Road. The distance was not the matter. It was the mission. The aim of every mother then was getting to know enough to save them picknee. Getting them better when they got sick as quickly as possible.

The healer my family use to deal with at Old Road, for a time, was one they call Ma Cilma. My parents would mostly go to look for her on a Thursday and come back on a Sunday. Sometimes when the man my grandmother had was in good mood, he would take them in the horse and cart up to Folly Hill and they would walk the rest of the journey. That ease the foot plenty and they would not have to stop on the journey to rest them foot. The woman healers never crave for money. Anything the people offer was the pleasure. My mother use to give Ma Cilma a bit when things florishing and sometimes a-half a bit or so when things bad. At other times nothing at all.

The Old Road People would apply different remedies at times . They wrap plantain sucker round the joints mainly round the wrist to take out pain. Exercise the fingers with the whole lemon to prevent them keeping the curve of the fork and the hoe stick. They drink the lemon water to clean the blood and also use lime and lemon skin to clean between the toes. The Healers best use for rum was to use it to wash from them knee to them toes.

Old Road healers would boil different bush and store them in jar pots. Ma Cilma at one time, have over twelve jar pots. When the sick come, the healers would have the remedy most of the time. They would just heat up the proper one and give the dose or the amount to take away. They would also know very well when the mixture stay long enough in the jar pots and would boil fresh ones. They use to boil fresh bush mostly on Saturdays. That was to get ready for the Sunday rush, the day when most people go for the many remedies. Mark you the dose then was not by the spoonful as the doctors prescribe nowadays. At that time then and part of my time, the dose was by the mouthful. One mouthful, two mouthful or how much mouthful the healer would tell the person to drink.

People back then seldom wait until they get sick to use certain remedy. They usually carry out a clean out process at certain periods. The older heads believe that to clean out the body prevent them from getting certain sickness. They would drink some sinklebible, or sana or wormgrass tea or inflamation bush, or cranderberry bush, crush beet or any remedy the healer would give them that can purge out the body.

My mother always say that my grand mother was always in a hurry to travel to Old Road after Ma Cilma open up she yie. In rain or sunshine she gone in search of the knowledge. It was there she get to know that to soak dry okra in water and gargle was good for sore throat and that the same dry okra pound to powder, mix in water and drink was good for the stomach. And that celery done the same way or properly chew-up-raw and swallow with water keep down heart burn. That is also good remedy for when a woman is in the way. The healers there would also recommend goat milk for the same purpose. People don't milk goat now in this land.

My mother have no idea that people could have sickness that could make them can't see too far, or make them see far and not close enough until she learn that from the Old Road people. Today, people know the sickness to be near-sightedness or far-sightedness. The remedy my mother pick up at Old Road for the people that have the near sightedness, was that they should use beet, green turnips, pusley or dandy-lion regularly. And that the remedy for the people that can see far but not near enough, is just simple, eat a thing they call sunflower seeds. She also preach morning and night that if people want to be able to see good when they come old, they

4. A pregnant woman.

130

must get in the habit of drinking raspberry juice, raw carrot water or chew them up and swallow with a few mouthful of water and clean the eye with bright eye bush water. No joke with that. As I see now, doctors give specs for both the near and the far sight sickness and that would be the end of that. But say me old Papa Sammy say, specs alone won't cure the problem. The young people will feel that the specs make them look good. They will gladly wear them, but the real cure or help for the sight, me believe, is to do what the older heads say along with the specs from the doctor, if you really need them.

The Old Road healers was the first my mother witness use their tongue and suck catarra out-a people yie. That was one of the things she always wish that she could do. She never develop the way nor the will to be able to do it. Nowadays, I hear people talk about glaucoma. I don't remember hearing 'bout that disease when I was growing up or when I pass mid-age. The word is new to me. Me hear that disease blind people. There was not too much blind people in my village. The most memorable one would be Arthur Mason. It was always a hard thing for anyone to put any tricks on him. Many people who didn't know him chose to do business with him because they think that they could fool him. That was not easy. Swapping horse was a regular thing. Try to swap blind man Mason a horse with a defect and see if you get through. Mason's test was to feel the horse all over the body. The final test was to feel in the mouth of the animal. His finger would tell if the swap should take place. When he approve, that was well-sounded. There was another blind man from Willikies. They call him Blind Doctor. He too was a superman. He use to walk from Willikies to the city all by himself. That village is some seven to eight miles away from the city. Blind Doctor would go exactly where he want to go without any help and back to Willikies on foot. He could tell when a villager or a friend was passing him on the road.

One of the memorable things my mother discover at Old Road, was the use of the Bellman Tree. I later get to know that the planters call the same tree Comfrey tree. Maybe that's why some people refer to it as the comforter. The right name I understand is the Golden seal. The new generation do not seem to know the value of it. It is mortally capital for bleeding ulcer and many more stomach and other complaints. Throw on the boiling water, let it cool and drink. Take a good cold cup full first thing in the morning and it will help to keep the pressure down. The tree use to grow all over the place. It would grow anywhere but those that grow in swampy area would have more healing power.

Nowadays, people chap them down and use them to make fire. What a Pity! All seem to vanish out of sight. The tree is a normally high tree and is known from the yellow flowers that shape like a bell. I hope that this blessed tree would be resurrected and the people would start to use it again. Some people use it for almost any sickness. It will also dry up heat and sores.

Freeman's Village people and many others in the north, use the eucalyptus bush as a remedy for cold and flu or just drink it as tea. At Old Road, there was at least another use for it. When the Old Road man pippie and they feel a little burning or discomfort, they would take a good drink to stop the burning and clean the track. And she learn there that the hair between the corn is good for cleaning the bladder. Just draw and drink like a tea. The man stringing nettle do the same thing. Another thing was that the people at Freeman's Village use to go and look honey just to drink it. It was fun to go and look honey, smoke out the bees and get a sting or two. The honey was for food. Kill the hunger and drink the water behind. But at Old road, my mother get to know that the healers use honey as remedy for dry and paxy skin, burns, sores and heat. They also use it to grease the hair and sometimes they would grease the whole body with it. Old Road people pung up[5] course salt as fine as they could get it and mix it with coconut oil to rub the joints. Salt in coconut oil is good, never mind what use you put it to.

The present generation and those to come will move on and never get to know the real power of the Old Road Healers. To talk

5. To crush.

about them now is trupitness. Big laugh for the people of today. But say after me their knowledge remain unbeaten. A real mystery. Back then at Old Road, when a man feel weaky-weaky and down, feel as if he can't tun shad off a coal; and at the same time, can't come up with what is wrong, the healers would first clean him out with what to them was best.

Then they would put him on raw vegetables like carrot, lettuce, spinach, tomato and green corn would not be left out. Chop the vegetable up and then mix them with honey and thyme and eat up. That with tizzan tea was a capital mixture. After all that, they would then give them a little pumpkin seed soup to tickle up the body. This land pass through drastic change with certain things. People of today throw-way the pumpkin seed. Take it from me, that is the best part of the pumpkin. The people in the south use to preserve the pumpkin seed to make sure that they have it when time come. In those days, a little pumpkin seed soup would put a man back on ee[6] foot. The yellow macaroni vine tea also make man feel good.

To me it was a little strange to understand that the people at Freeman's Village and in the larger part of the land eat cucumber with salt and pepper while the southern villages, mainly Old Road, mix the cucumber with honey and lime juice. To them, the salt on the cucumber was craziness. In our village and the surroundings, sage tea was the capital remedy for baby gripe. At Old Road, the healers make it doubly capital. They add ginger to the sage tea, and that was the remedy for the griping stomach for big and little. Only the dose separate them.

The use of the bush we call Privy bush was not known to many of the people in the north of the island. But we know from the Old Road people that to draw privy bush tea, add little salt from the salt pond and gaggle, was a capital remedy for hoarseness and sore throat. The healers at old Road also use raspberry to clean the tongue. They also use salt purge to gaggle and that heal the tongue as well.

6. His

Once upon a time, Old Road people hardly knock up over bread, dumplin or flour food. Other people would eat the usual bread, dumplin or potato with little bush tea in the morning or night. The usual breakfast for Old Road people was raw ground nut and garlic tea or what ever and the garlic tea. To them, that was much better and helpful to the stomach than anything else. Freeman's Village people and the surroundings would parch the ground nut and use it just for pleasure. The Old Road way was new-new and strange to my mother and her family. Healer, Ma Cilma use to say, nah mine wa de sickness, no one will go wrong if they use the garlic. I believe that if some of the young people use garlic tea before they rush off to the doctor today, they would get relief from the complain and save their money. Sometimes what doctors give, would not work as fast or as long. I am not calling down the doctors, not one bit, but I know for certainty that plenty people rush to them because their mind trouble them. If they would just have some faith, most times, they would hardly need doctors, particularly when they are in their youthful days. A little garlic tea is always helpful whether in the morning or night. The woman healers tell my mother that she must never be afraid. She can't do any wrong by using it for the inside or the outside. Don't boil garlic at anytime. Just draw it. I mean just bust up the sprig and pour on the boiling water and let it cool to suit the throat. To boil garlic is to rob it of the real power. Just to chew the garlic and swallow with a few mouthful of water is good-good. Just that, keep away the gas and the hungry feeling. Garlic will make the gas pass out a the right place and would not stay back to cause pain. To force out gas like thunder, just drink inflammation bush, gas bush, french thyme and garlic all draw together.

My mother never forget the time when she went to Old Road for the first time. What stick up so much in her memory was what the healer, Ma Cilma give she and she mother for dinner. The dinner was boil green fig and raw garlic, with St. John's bush tea behind. That vomit them and Ma Cilma say a dirty the stomach dirty and the garlic cleaning it. Ma Cilma tell them to try the garlic until they get accustom to it. When they get back home, they try to eat the garlic. They put up with some trouble until they get use to the taste. They also learn that to crush the garlic and put it on sores and heat, was something that her villagers were glad to know. My mother was a sound believer in the Old Road remedy. She always tell us that one cup of garlic tea make the blood flow like how God say it to flow. Everyone of she picknee must drink that when she say. When Picknee nash[7] and ketch cold quick, garlic tea was one of the remedy them mothers use to bring round the picknee. The garlic tea also help to harden nash picknee as well.

It was the custom of the people in the southern villages to put a sprig of garlic in the plait hair. That, they claim, was to keep a bad jumbie[8] from hitting that person in the head. When someone was sick, they would also tie a few sprigs in a bit of cloth, on the ankle and around the wrist, in addition to that already in the head for the same reason.

Today, the doctor is all over town with wide open doors and young people rush them down for a simple headache. They just cannot do without the phensic or the asprin. In my day, there was not such a comfort. The Old Road remedy for that was simple, simple. The man with the headache would put his head in the woman lap. She would put her hand on the forehead for sometime, then press below the ears with the big and index fingers of both hands at the same time for a while, then hold the back of the head with the palm of the right hand for a time. Man would fall asleep in the woman lap. Headache-garn. When the woman have the headache, she would put she head in the man lap and the same remedy apply. Give a little garlic tea after the sleep if you like. Headache take long, long to come back after that. The young people take the pill, tan little bit them start cry for the same headache. So pill don't cure headache. Again and again, me can't stop say so, when some of the young peo-

7. Weak and sick often.
8. Spirit.

ple of this generation hear me talk, they say that I know a whole tun.[10]

If the people now could get the chance to meet one healer or to hear my mother talk bout the Old Road people, they would certainly find out that me Papa Sammy know little bit-just-little-bit. Those woman healers was clean gone[11] and me can't stop say so. Back then, the Bakkra doctors that come out of school could not match them. The doctors today, may feel they know all, but they have a long way to go to match them healers, who never see a school door. The healers, have some natural powers that them doctors and other people do not want to hear about. And to me, that is the key, the real key, with the knowledge. Man will always increase his knowledge. Little lower than angels, he is - will do wonders - but a body is a body in any age. Doctors would have to accept that natural healing power of the healers is also wonderful knowledge and the two kinds should work side by side. Nothing will be better.

The Antigua Bakkra in this land use to overload them stomach. That make them sick fast. Back then, it would never cross their mind that a good living a kill them. The bakkra doctors if they know it, could not drunk tell them to stop the ravenous eating and drinking. On top of that, most of the Bakkra doctors carry the name, but many times could not tend to their own people properly. Healers use to do anything to bring comfort and lengthen man life Massa will do anything to live on and on. One, Massa Bertie of Winthrop Estate had a son that was sickly. The young fella sick-lack-a-dog. As usual, Massa doctors try everything available, but young Jack Bertie remain sick-sick-sick. Massa Bertie, after all, swallow his pride and decide to try a healer. His own doctors get against him because he decide as the last try to get the healer. He get on his horse and cart and cross the land from Winthrope to Old Road. Winthrope have its own healer, but the practice then was to use people from a distance. Keep nosey neighbour out of them business. Old Road was the pick then.

9. Moments later the headache returns.
10. To be full of knowledge.
11. To have genius like quality.

Between the 1850's and 1870's or so, the people use to have a woman name Ma Jukey as the best healer at Old Road. Massa Bertie want the best and he find she. Me think that Ma Jukey would be the proudest woman on earth then just because a Bakkra come to she to try and heal his picknee. Anyone could just imagine how that was big-big subbon to Ma Jukey. My mother use to say that Ma Jukey was a stern woman. She never coax anybody unless that body was a new born picknee. No orders with a soul who nah tek heed[12] Some people want to get heal but give trouble to take the medson. Do wa-she-say or don't ask she for help. Bakkra or no bakkra, she make that known before she and her daughter Vickey jump in Massa Bertie cart and leave Old Road for Winthropes.

Daughter Vickey must walk in her mother shoes. Nar lef she behind fu nutton. After they put themself together, the best known healer and her daughter follow Massa Bertie to Winthropes Estate. From Old Road to Winthrope is from south shore to the north shore, and that was a new land for Vickey and her mother.

All the sick young Jack Bertie sick, and could not even move, it did not take Ma Jukey anytime to find out what was causing the problem. A bone in his back slip out. The youngster nyam too much, get too fat and could not walk. Ma Jukey put him on garlic tea, vegetables, horse oats and rice. The order was not to touch the rum, not even the slightest piece of meat, no chicken, ee worse with the egg, no fish, no pickle food. Pig meat was the go, but Healer, Ma Jukey say that was the worse meat. Too lardy.[14] And you wouldn't believe me, he couldn't eat anything make out of flour. Not even a drop of milk he was to drink. In those days people say milk was the perfect food. He was not to start eat before mid-morning and no eating after sundown. Full stop!. Only the duck weed tea or little donkey milk he could drink after sunset. That was for the short blowing.

The young sick man take a while before he could understand all that he could not devour. Just to ease up off of the eating a little was the biggest punishment for any bakkra. The sick man could not

12. Not following instructions.
14. Too fat.

move round so he could not go and devour what he like and that was it.

My mother recall the story that in a short time and her short time mean, by next two to three moonlight, the sick man loose enough weight and fat that Ma Jukey could fit the bone back in place again. And that was that. She put her ear on the young man chest and was not too happy over what she hear. And so she put him on one peggy mouth pepper every other day for a week. Clean up the heart. Young Bertie start to climb upon horse back, again. After that he did not want to hear a word about his own english doctors. Then there was a four to five year old son for the same Bakkra that have all the chat on earth, mouth lack-a-bell but would-n't walk. All creeping he decide to do. Ma Jukey fix he up too. She boil up barakada bush, cojoe root bush, love bush, french thyme and trangman bush and bark the picknee kin with the mixture as hot as he could bear it. When she done, she bang the picknee on his foot with some fresh trangman bush and tell him with meaning, - git up! Me say git up! And, lea-me-tell-you, the picknee git up and walk. Ma Jukey was queen for Winthrope Estate. But according to my mother, the Old Road top healer put on another Old Road show on the Winthrope Bakkra. She use broom-broom bush and sweep out the house. She and daughter dust every ledge and corner. After that, she soak lavinder bush and dutch grass in water and wash down the place. Then she smoke out the house with three corner smoke. What the Old Road people call the three corner smoke was when they burn three different kinds of bush together.

Ma Jukey after cleaning out the house say she prayers in she own way. And according to the older head, bad luck vanish. At Old Road, the people use to burn the same bush in a new house before they take up lodging in it. Parson burn incense in bakkra buff. Healer burn bush in the poor man house. In the end is the spirit and the heart. She find plenty memory bush at Winthrope and she give the memory bush tea, to help the memory.

Ma Jukey and daughter became the bossom friend of bakkra Bertie family. As usual, the Bakkra want she for themself. He want

Ma Jukey to live at Withrope and not to go back to Old Road. Ma Jukey say no Massa. That part of the land did not have enough trees and water. The area was also too hot for her. She miss she home, she people and she convenience.

In the midst of all the excitement, yong Jack Bertie have yie on Ma Jukey daughter. When they did not go to Winthrope, he would go to old Road to look for her regularly. Next thing, he find such a sweetness in a she, that he go and tell his people that he was going to take Vickey and make wife. Lord have mercy! That mash-up the friendship instantly. Everything 'pwoil! Massa Bertie order them off Winthrope with speed. Ma Jukey and daughter not to cross foot 'pon Winthrope again.

Wa-papa say no mean a thing to picknee.[15] No one could talk enough to get him to leave Ma Jukey daughter alone. Young Jack Bertie left his fathers house and go to live at Vernons Estate with friends. Nearer to the gal and further from Winthrope. Old Bertie realize that he was drifting his own picknee. He change and stop being outwardly bitter about the love affair and start to nice-up with son and sweetheart. Invite mother and daughter back to Winthrope. All of a sudden, back like peas in a pod again. Massa Bertie start to build a new buff for son and sweetheart. Everything was set. Son get his own way. As soon as new buff done build wedding was the rumour. And Vickey seeing the best of her days.

But in the midst of the pleasure come the trouble. One Saturday morning the sad news come, that Vickey drown in Withrope Bay. The explanation was she and Massa Bertie was out in the early morning bay and she drop down into a sucking hole. Young Jack Bertie feel um. He nearly go crazy. He was no use to himself for days. The father take the body back to Old Road and explain to the mother with all the pity he could. Young Bertie could not even follow the body. He reached sometime after and see where they lay her. He lament to Vickey mother that it was the only time Vickey go early bay with his father and only when the cry come out that she drown, he know that she was not in the house. And the rea-

15. To disobey parental rule and pursue own path.

son why he feel so bad was that some of his friends keep mocking him saying "You Vickey married to shark - you Vickey married to shark". At times, they would yell at him and say, "shark teeth sharp but not sharp enough for you Vickey".

The father later ship young Jack Bertie to England for him to ketch himself, forget the scene and to get a new start. My mother said before he actually leave he went to Old Road to bid Ma Jukey goodbye and to thank her for putting him back on his foot again. During all this time, my family was living at Vernons Estate. They know the Bertie family and was also a friend of Ma Jukey and her daughter. The Old Road Connection. I remember my mother use to say how the father Massa Bertie grow to love Vickey and that she sure that he himself could not eat well for the misfortune of poor Vickey.

I did not come into the world yet when this story happen. But life has a way to make you learn new things. I was only working with the Goodwins for just over five years when a young white Englishman by the name of Bill Bertie show up to be an overseer. The Goodwins tell me to show him around. I did just that. The young man seem to want to work in the climate.

It was not long after the walk around that R.S.D. Goodwin ask me if I ever hear the story of a white man who drown a black woman to stop his son from disgracing himself. I did not understand him. What he wants to tell me is that young Bill Bertie was the grandson of Massa Bertie, the man that drown a black healer daughter to stop young Bill's father from marrying her.

R.S.D. always say in those days whenever a white man wants to marry a black woman, the result was death. He talks about his own family. A member of his own family want to marry a black woman. He was hells bent. He said no one could stop him. He will give up the family for this. People a people- black, white, red or mahogany.

His own friends fix him. They decide no disgrace must come on them. We must end this thing. He was taken out to sea which

was a regular thing. They push him overboard. When he hold to
the edge of the boat, they chopped his fingers off. He was gone.
Case close! Goodbye! That's over. And so the Goodwins were
right.

10
SCORCH EARTH:
An orgy of crimes
and destruction

One of the biggest regret I have of late is not holding on to some of the pictures, paintings and books the Goodwin family had and do away with. Whatever do not belong to me, I don't trouble. That is one of the biggest lesson I teach my children and the people around me. Even the books, paintings, scraps and other things that was to be thrown out, I did not take. Only now as I look back and see that they are all gone, the thought flash back in me that I should walk with some. The record they use to keep would be useful to the people of this land until life last. R.S.D. Goodwin always say that certain members of his family was in charge of the committee to put the record in the Antigua Blue Book for many years. He was personally responsible for the true record to go in the Blue Book from 1915 to 1941. He explain to me that the name Blue Book have nothing to do with the colour. It is the record book of the Colony. I cannot remember seeing the Blue Book at his house. But I get me belly full from the family record book. That was a book. It would be like precious stone today. It was in that book I see that it was the Governor that use to say who should become priest for the Anglican Church. The same book mention how much money they should get. When my eyes behold that, I laugh and laugh, because I then know that they have everybody well fool off. They preach that it was God that call the priests to preach the word of God. Up to now, I still have to laugh. They preach the Governor word. The word of the Mother Country. At one time, the governor use to pay the Boss priest 22 pound sterling a month: That was big big money: I don't know if anybody would believe me, all I know I did not see wrong. I look at it again and again until the whole thing soaked in-a-me[1]. Some people now and over the years, believe in them priest, too bad. But I know long time that God call no priest as they say. They use to talk plenty for the Governor and the bakkra. They use to have the most say. That is the truth.

I learn that the early Planters, before the 17th century cut up Antigua into parishes, and they start with five. Some planters want as much as eight. They then settle with six. St. John's Parish up to now is the largest. St. Mary follow and the next to that, is St. Paul and then St. Phillip. The sixth and smallest is St. George and the second smallest happen to be St Peter.

The Goodwin paper show that between 1707 and 1750, Antigua reach the peak with the number of Sugar Estates. There was about 175, to 185 of them at the time of the Freedom. There would be some small holdings in between. The correct number, I never hear about.

The Parish of St Phillip was busy, busy. That parish use to have at one time thirty-seven estates. It had then, about 200 drawn carriages. That would include horse and cart, cattle cart, buggy and extension. The Sugar Mills were either driven by the wind or by cattle.

1. It cannot be forgotten.

The new freedom bring new and serious work problems for the old massas. The moving away of the free people from the estates did not affect the running of the estates in any real serious manner until the Bakkra could not satisfy some of the most important workers. The big cry from massa over the moving away of the ex-slaves from the estates in the first place was because of the loss of control over them. The estates would still function properly even though they shed so much tears. But when the Wheel Wright, the Carpenter, and Cooper and the Blacksmith start to act up, that was the serious part of the business. Those workers, all of a sudden, begin to enjoy the freedom just like the others. That was a bad, bad one for the bakkra. That was subbon else! The bakkra brok them neck to satisfy them.

Back then, the thing the estates used to hold water and to feed animals out of, was the tub or the trough. These are made of barrel staves or wood. The Cooper was the man to fix the water tub. The tub must keep in the shade at all times and full of water if not it would split up.

The estate owners could not do without the Cooper. He was a big man. So too, was the same thing with the Carpenter. He build and repair the cart and other things. Let me tell you the bakkra could not do without the Wheelwright to make the cart wheel, neither could they do without the blacksmith to fit the band round the wheel. If the horse want on shoe only the Blacksmith could put it on. Without the shoe, the bakkra could not ride the horse on them flinstone road for long. The animal would become lame and would go out of commission. When these workers start to taste the freedom, it cause a major turning point in the thinking of the Planters. Man start to follow woman and sleep off more and more in the village with them. Because of that, the bakkra could not depend on them to turn up for work when needed. Massa plan the thing out. They set up workshops for them near some of the villages. The blacksmith shop was always outside the village. Most of the Coopers and the Carpenters workshops were put in the village itself.

The Goodwin record book mention that their family own 248 slaves at one time, before the freedom. Between 1835 and 1850, the ex-slaves living on their estates dwindle to less than fifty. The slave houses were nearly all empty. The real problem start when the tradesman start to enjoy them freedom like the other people. Cart wheel was there to fix and Bakkra could not move up and down as they want. They use to walk up and down in their house like them haunted when the man to fix them was enjoying himself in the village with his woman. That was the situation on nearly all of the estates.

Some estates had more labour problems than others. Betty's Hope estate was the one to get hit the hardest. That plantation use to take on almost every business in the land, from making coffin to clothes, to belts to shoes. The famous estate make parts of all descriptions, for cart, for horse, for plough for everything. The only tanner shop of any consequence in the land could barely keep open. Hardly any new saddle to replace old ones could be found at one point. Horses sadle was running low. The do-all Betty's Hope could not make shoes for the big foot bakkra that can't find them size. No where in the land could there be found any estate that could curry comb and meign comb[2] horse better than Betty's Hope. That estate has the fame to curry comb and meign comb the governor horse since the time of a governor they call Governor Parks. Betty's Hope hold that fame until horse come out of vogue. The story was when the people really begin to smell the freedom, not even govenor horse get the usual attention. Spree first then anything after.

The Goodwins blame the women for the problems. Later, I find out the reason in the family record book. According to the book, when nearly 17,000 people live across the land on new sites in 1863-64, man make up only five and one half thousand. The man kind roam between living on the estates and the free villages.

Few people if any are alive today that can tell of the giant Corn Mill. That's the mill that hush the corn to feed the animals. The Planters would do anything to keep the giant Corn Mill driver.

2. To clean-up the skin of the horse.

Sugar production in those days could not take place without animals. That was from start to stop. Back then, the animal doctor would have plenty more calls than the human doctor. Corn mix up with fussie and water keep the animals going. That was one of the main feed for them. The mill itself was driven by animals. The animals were hooked in a shaft and they travel round and round to crush the corn. The corn mill driver was considered to be a King for sugar production. No animal, no sugar. When workers like them start to stall, look out! That-a-trouble. The bakkra bend and bend to suit them. They bend and take it easy just because they could not come up with a plan. The bakkra did not know how to handle the situation. Them fraid of riot. Them fraid the people might drive them out of the land. The other big fear I believe would be the fear of the reverse. That is, the people may put them to work like how they use to work them. That feeling would have to cross some of the bakkra mind from time to time. At that time, most of the Planters and their families were well fortified in the land. Not another place they would go although their heart and soul was always in the Mother Country. Most would find it hard to pack up and go. In any land, people would always go and come. Those who remain in this one, had the worry of seeing more and more ex-slaves move from the estates and out from under bakkra control. It was hard on the bakkra when the weather was the problem and any other thing for that matter.

Weather is always a problem for the massas. A thing they could not control. But when the people give problems that they were unable to find the ready answer to, they would take it to heart. The massas at that time find it a hard job to divide the people even though no one was around for them to look up to. That generation that live through slavery know no divide. The pain and peril was the bond. The very most of them were determine to keep away from them former massas until death. Don't worry to think that the massas did not try every trick in the book to divide up the people. The bulk of them hold firmly to their heart's desire.

Greater effort to win control of former slaves and them pick-nee get very serious on the part of the bakkra. Between 1863 and 1864 quite a good number of the population loose them life. It was about that same time or little after that a good portion of the head cullian for the putting up of the free villages pass on. According to my mother and other people, almost all of them dead the same way. They take in with gripe and vomit and then pass out. Ma Sophie, Isabella and Gloria of Garden Estate dead the same week. They were 'trang, trang Methodist. They even build a trash house Methodist church at Garden Estate. All three was head and head in not working for Massa again. They set up the village Hopeful East. In that same period, Amelia of Free-Fu-All and Trotty from Free Wilbur Village just take-in with vomiting and move on. The same thing happen to Natlee of Freemans Village. Those were just from the surroundings.

My family was still living at Vernon's Estate. The sudden death of the people from the same thing cause a big alarm. My mother lamented that the same cry at Moroe was the same cry at Briggin. Some say that it was fever that kill the people. Others say it was poison. The fever and the deaths did not trouble the estate people who decide to stay with their massa. My mother on her Bible oath say that a poison they poison the people. It look too pointed. Some blame the bakkra picknee they call the "colour-red". They poison the water that some people in the village have to drink.

Fire start to be one of the main weapon use against the black people to force them back on the estates. Lady Jumbia give plenty strength to my mother argument. She say about a year after the deaths, some village have fire night after night. As often as the people put up the house, another would go up in flames. My mother again say that a the "colour-red" burn down the place. Them half white bakkra picknee always want to put themselves in the bakkra shoes. The bakkra never own them. At that period with the deaths and the fire, the "colour-red had" a fairer face than the "colour-red round" slavery time. The reason for that was, the bakkra was making more picknee with more half white than the black, black woman. After slavery more bakkra spread out themselves with more woman outside the bakkra colour. The "colour-red" use to show just as much hate, or even more for the ex-slaves than the ex-slave owner themselves. Their jealousy was bitter, bitter against the village people. Up to 1866, villages were still going up. The planters, up to then, could not come up with a plan of how to handle the ex-slaves. What to do to check them speed? That was the nighmare that look as if it had no ending. But lo' and behold almost exactly what the massas in this land was mortally afraid of take place in Jamaica.

The big rumor in the land then was that the people in Jamaica disobey the Queen, refused to work for their massas and instead go into town, and make trouble. And them that did not meet their death get such a licking, that they remain speechless for days. And those that lucky to reach back home meet ashes instead of house. They have to rush to the very massas that they did not even want to see and the massas rescue them without a murmur. They were glad to go back for the shelter on the very estate that they turn them backs on. The news was slow in those days. My mother say that she was eleven years old at the time, when the news grip this land. That was some two years after it happened. She say when the Jamaica trouble spread through the land properly, the priests and the parsons that use to have a little sympathy for the people take the planters side full square. Priest and parson say they want no riot in this land. They take the lead and warn that the same thing that happen in Jamaica was bound to happen in this land if the people continue to disobey and refuse to live and work with their massas. After the news break through, things get real hot. My mother say almost every night after that, some village somewhere catch a fire and when the people run from the fire, them run into some fierce stone firing and nobody could tell a who. Planters from top to bottom did not waste a single moment to pile on the pressure on the people. Them and the priests and all the bakkra, along with the colour red, use that Jamaican problem to crush the ex-slaves in the land. There was not a drop of mercy shown because they want to get back the control they badly want over the people.

The bulk of the people who know what slavery was all about and would fight back, was old then. Those who would rather die than return to them one-time owners would be too weak to fight. And don't forget, a lot of the fighters were gone off the scene. The priests and parsons take charge with the bible and the hymn book. While the ex-slaves and them picknee come dotish and forget bout everything that mean good to them.

The generation living in the late 1860's would get the hardship of the slave life second hand.[4] Some would not think that it could happen to them. Others would not care what happen. There would be a good portion of the picknee of the ex-slaves that would not get the stout-heart against the ex-slave owners as their parents would always have. Throughout my life, I see it happen again and again that some picknee don't care too hoots what happen to them ma. Some would not even claim them. The bakkra know long time that it would be easier to get the young people to live under them. Only a little bit of them would be as determined as their parents. The older heads was the problem. The young people did not face the real hardship and so some would believe the bakkra more than their parents. They would not look back. All they do was to honour and obey the same bakkra.

The bakkra head never stop trying to find the answer to regain their control. Ratta fu-gat trap. Trap na fu-gat ratta.[5] The new generation of the 1860's did not learn that lesson. The Methodist and Moravian preachers who help the people in the earlies, would also be old and weak or gone. The Preachers in the 1860's and 1870's were far different to those in the early years after slavery. The young people would not believe that estate life could

4. The Post slavery generation did not bear the suffering of slavery and so became complacent.
5. Revenge never dies.

149

be that hard. No one could preach enough. They did not suffer it like them parents.

I don't know if anybody today heard of the dying wish of Father Darius, the Barbados Anglican priest that take over St Phillip's Anglican church sometime in the mid 1860's. According to R.S.D. Goodwin, when he lay dying, his last words to the people who gather round his bedside was, "Don't go astray! To live with your massa is best." The topic of his first sermon in Antigua was, "Life would be better for the ex-slaves if they return to their massas." That was his message. Talking of the earthly massas. He was like a champion out of Barbados. The Darius phrase that live long after his death was, "Don't be fools! Get under the roof, Massa knows best." The Goodwins use to say that the Darius words were powerful in prayers and nearly in all the ways of the time. It help them.

The big joke the planters use to give about Father Darius was that he was the sharpest Anglican Priest from way he come from. He could maketh a picknee one na well out before one in. One in every thirteen months and that he end up with nine picknee in thirteen years of his marriage. He was not able to perform much in Antigua. He pass on when the tenth picknee was on the way. And he was in the land for less than a year.

A parson that was hard, hard on the people for them to return to the plantation was a Parson Malone. Lady Jumbia usually refer to him as Debble Malone. He accuse the women healers of the sick hark of working obeah. He drive them with speed off Hawksbill compound and burn down the sick hark in broad daylight. He supervise the fire and get his gang to throw what was left from the fire into the sea. The women healers ran for shelter in the nearby village. That village was also set on fire. The sick, lame and the well, run for their life. They get peace only when they decide to follow Debble Malone and return to the nega house on the Five

---

6. He was impregnating his wife year after year.

Islands Estate. At one time, Freeman's Village was down to three houses. Freetown Village down to five. My mother always say that she believe that it was the Methodist church in those villages that save them from complete destruction. She also say that by 1870 or so, all the new villages that the people put up round Vernons and Parham were gone. If there was any house, no one was in them. My family who was living on Northsound say there was no room to hold people at Northsound at that horrible period. Room or no room, the people had not a choice. They must find themselves on anyone of the plantation. That was all massa want. The people fall in line under them again. I think that it was the saddest moment in the lifetime of this land. The pressure was on terrible, terrible. The young gals bear the most chaff. It was bad, bad for them. Circumstance force them to give in to any man who come to rape them. Even if they would fight off man after man, they could not resist all. No longer could the people claim the ten acres that the Queen have on every estate as was the case just after the freedom. The argument of the priest was that the Queen take back the land and return it to the Massas, therefore every man, woman and picknee must find shelter on the estates. What the bakkra and the "colour-red" people did not do, the hurricane do in 1871 and plantation life start full force all over again.

At the beginning of the 1870's all but three of the villages vanish off the land. Standing was Freeman's Village, Liberta and Freetown. They were not in anyway firm. It was a shaky thing. It look as if they could merge them into any nearby estate at anytime in that period. The older heads think it was Providence that really keep them. And if it was not for Providence that keep them, there would not be a trace of the near seventy villages that was put up by the free people of this land after slavery. All the old slave plantations now come village. What a shame. There is now the Bolans Village. Where Massa Bolans get village from? Tell me? How come slave massa Bendal and Potter and Swetes, Jennings and them so get

151

village? Everywhere, village carry the name after the old slave massas plantation. And our enlightened people follow the same road up
to now. What a pity. A guess they don't know better, a situation
that bothers me.

One of my biggest concern is that Massa Willikie get village
too. The ordinary people could not call the name Willikie. Two
Willikie brothers come to the land some time near the end of the
century. Frank Willikie was manager of Rooms plantation for some
10 to 12 years. He and his family occupy three or four houses at
Rooms and the planters refer to the place as "Up Willikies". The
family left the land after the turn of the century for Merica. The
Goodwins say they leave in vexation because Frank Willikie did not
get the expected job at the new sugar factory that begin operation in
1905 or their about. People use to say that Frank Willikie laugh too
much with his fungie. As a result a grain of hair has never grown in
his face.[7]

Extreme vengence from the bakkra and them, lackadaisical-
ness from the young generation, all that with the constant pressure
from all sides force the people back on the estates. The old people
who live through that time dead with a whole lot of sorrow and
grief in their hearts. To me it was by far the most brutal period in
our history and up to now the voices are quiet about it.

7. A local saying when a man's face is smooth and does not grow a grain
of hair.

11

THE GREAT CONTRAST:
Depending on Massa and not themselves

y Mother always harp and harp that between the mid-1870's up to well into the 1900's, this place was a real filthy land. Dirty, plenty dirty, the worst she live through. She would say her tongue can't find words to tell how it was. Not even if she try. It was not like in slavery, or when the people live in the villages for the little time. Far, far from what it was then. In salvery and in the thirty-year period of the free village life, people use to dig holes and empty the kooka[1] and other dirty things in them. After the return to estate life the people throw the kooka and other dirty things in the open. That would be mostly at the back of the plantation, some distance away in the bush from the last nega house. That was the kooka Bendal.[2] Although the Kooka Bendal. would be a good distance from the last nega house, the people could not escape the bad smell. It would be worse when the breeze blow in a direction direct to the dwellings. The people were all bundled

---

1. Human waste.
2. Uncovered place for the disposal of human waste and filth.

up on one another. I believe that particular state of living was part of the revenge on the people for leaving the plantation in the first place.

The world is changing much faster now than how most people believe. Most of the younger people no longer make time to hear the older heads talk life over as use to happen at moonlight nights and 'round the fireside or even just to chat away the time. To give jokes or talk tory or just to meet together and talk, ease the frustration and the pressure that normally accompany hard life. Sometimes the older people would talk us to sleep and they would come back with a new tory[3] again and again. Any amount of 'tory was around in those days and so was the different argument. Think of anything like, which estate have the most red mouth people. Nearly every soul would say North Sound. Arguments also about where have the most big foot people. That was Potters Estate, but some would say Liberta. Where have the best looking gals some would say Hawksbill, others would say Vernons. Parham too was hot in the running. There would even be bigger arguments too, over which kooka Bendal was the filthiest. At one time, my mother use to be on her bible oath that no kooka Bendal was as filthy as that of Weirs Estate. The smell stop her from deciding to live at Weirs. That was the reason for her to leave North Sound to Jonas. But Kenneth Coull, one of her man friend, always try to convince her that the kooka Bendal at Weirs Estate was not the worst. Coull's argument was that he roam from estate to estate and up to then he live on twenty-two of them and that my mother could not be in her right mind to name Weirs Estate as the filthiest. Coull use to call estates like Parsons Maul, Dunbars, Briggins, Lighfoot, Swetes, Cades Bay, Christian Valley, Cotton and Donovan as being far more filthy than Weirs. But anyone can just imagine what life in this land was like when the top massas of the land, the Goodwins, the Foots, the Tudways and others declare that Glanvilles smell was the very worst in the land. According to the Goodwins, their own family own and run it at that time. One Guss Goodwin, they say, never

3. Story

keep himself clean. Anyone could imagine what the nega house and the surroundings was like. He was dead to anything name cleanliness. The Goodwins I work with have it to say that anytime they get close to Glanville, the smell would follow them for a long, long distance away. They would never pass near the Glanville nega house for all the money in the world.

Between the 1860's and the 1880's the population of the land run down. The Bakkra could do without so many nega people round them. I can't say what the population was like, from year to year between that period but the Goodwin family record book have it to say, that the population drop from 38,000 in 1851 to 33,000 in 1878 and that was the period when quite a number of women dead out from child's birth. The book also have it that the population pick up a little in the 1890's and run down as low as 30,000 after the turn of the twentieth century.

In days of long ago and even up to now many nega people would be lucky to see the Governor. Even if they happen to see him they could not pick him out. The ones that would know about the governors would be the big shot bakkra and their kind. They were the ones that would generally control the movement of the Governors. From time to time, the governor would have service in Big church and there he would talk his piece. The big bakkra would take him round only to places where they want him to see. They would keep any governor well away from the nega houses, the kooka bendals and any place like those. If the Governor happen to butt up on anything bad, the bakkra would blame the poor people. Bet you life that!

Governor Haynes Smith come to the land towards the end of the 1880's. Haynes Smith did not take too long to detect bad smell around St. John's city. A smell that he just could not take. Somehow he found out that the bad smell was coming from the many kooka bendals in and around the town. Except for the sea on the west end of town, Villa, Gambles, Woods, Ottos and Grays Estates form an arch around the city. Thick bush and sugar cane fields separate these estates from the town. Lonely roads with sugar cane fields on all sides lead to the city. The thick bush and canefields could not stop the bad smell from reaching the city from the kooka bendal of the encircling estates. Haynes Smith could not escape the smell particularly when the wind blow a little more rapid. The city dwellers too got their own kooka bendal. At least one was near Eve Garden burial ground near the sea. One was where we now call Michael Village and another at the end of North Street. The big houses use to have shallow latrines. They would hire a man from time to time to dig a new hole. So too there were many horse stables all over the town. One was at Country Pond on East Street, another was at the bottom of St. Mary's Street. A big one at the public works and inside government house yard. There was one at the market down Kings Wharf and people keep other animals too. There was the animal smell and the usual pockets of flies and mosquitoes that accompany that kind of living.

The bakkra in this land use to live with the feeling that the open koola Bendal was far away from them. And even if they smell a little bad smell now and again they could live with it. It won't hamper them that badly. To them, it should not cause any alarm. The smell make Haynes Smith cry out. He tell them just how he feel. They were all in the same cart with all the other people. Everybody nose hole pull in the same air, was his argument. Fever is for everybody. He describe St. John's as a place boxed in with sugar cane fields and bad smelling corpse.

Governor Haynes Smith right away start to tackle the sanitation problem. He put the Board of Health back together. He also bring in slab buckets to receive what he call the night soil from the city houses and the Board of Health workers would replace the slab buckets a-foreday morning. They carry the loaded buckets on their heads to Rat Island. That was where the Governor decide to dump the kooka in holes dig for that purpose. A portion of the city household would also have their own man that they could call on to empty their buckets. There was a dead dead secret about the people who was doing that job. Even if people happen to see them they could not easily detect them. They cover the whole head and face right down below the chin with a piece of cloth and two holes expose the eyes. They also tie the end of the cloth around the neck to prevent the wind blowing it over the head. The cloth was usually white in colour and mostly made from flour bags.

Down Rat Island was the home for the cocobay people.[5] They use to call it the Lepper colony. Plenty cocobay people was in the land. The cocobay people nearly take off a piece of cloud when they find out that the Governor give orders to dump kooka on them place. A whole tun a them over one hundred march up town with their cutlass and stick to see the Governor. Some ride donkeys but the majority on foot. Man, they maketh a racket. They behave like real outlaw. So them move on so them shout! No more kooka dung by ah-we. Not dun dey! "ar-we go pit high and lick low." When the business people recognize that a cocobay people let-loose, they shut down town right away and get under covers. The Governor close the dump one time. No argument with cocobay people. By the time they reach back to Rat Island, the hole done shut in, ram tight and dump transfer to land belonging to Villa Estate.

After the Govenor talk about cleaning up the city, the estates that form the ring around the city stop using open kooka bendal.

On a New Year's Sunday some time in the early 1890's Governor Haynes Smith tell the planters attending Big church service that they must not wait any longer to start to prepare for the new century. According to some planters, one of Haynes Smith regular statement was, the proper thing for the massas to do was to prepare well in time for the new century. No one he said should expect to carry the same way of life of the old century into the new. He also warned that the subjects of the mother country could not expect to continue to have beautiful flower gardens around their buffs and just a foot away from them, the Negro filth. It is folly to think that all are not in the same cart.

4. Well before the sun rise.
5. People who suffer from Leprosy.

The governor began a serious effort to improve the country. He tell his Anglican big shot bakkra that they will have to begin to embrace the poor ex-slaves and their off springs. If they fail to start urgently, the Church of England would certainly be left behind in the new century. Haynes Smith saw the growing challenge from the Catholics and urge Anglicans to start sharing food and clothing to the hungry like the Catholics. The other thing was that Haynes Smith had great difficulty understanding the tongue of the people who work at government house in his time. He could not depend on his groom to take a letter to the right soul, not even the ABC they know. The Labouring people at government house was dortish far beyond what Haynes Smith expected. The dortishness compel him to change the school week from two days to five, get more teachers and increase them money. He ask the church men to get down to business and teach the people the Queen's English. He recommend that the government take over the education from the church. I think the year was 1892 or thereabout when these changes start to take place. It was also in the early 1890's that midwives[6] come to the Island from England to deal with the poor people. He put a mid-wife in every district and on the large estates. They use to live most-ly in part of the church school. Another charge Haynes Smith give to the planters was that they should dig any hole that can hold water, plant more food and double up on the rearing of live stock for the new century.

Up to 1891, Nega man live with whatever hair God grow on their head and in their face. Man use to comb back the hair and sometimes tie it with a piece of string. Pickenega, gal and boy, use to plait their hair the same way. Some of the English bakkra would shave their beard a little with the hollow ground razor, but only a few chimb them head. Governor Haynes Smith ask that the men chimb up and shave up to meet the new century.

At that time, most people resist the governor. All of us do resist change, even if it is right. People would always test the change

6. A person trained to assist women in chidbirth.

but gradually and surely, one after the other will follow. Don't mine how slowly, they would fall in line. The town people obey the governor long before those out of town. In fact, some people think that the governor was talking only to the town man and not to them in the country and on the plantations. Cutting the hair off the head and shaving the face, present the new brand look of the town man. Those that join lodges and some other big shot people obey the governor with speed. One thing for sure the climbing of the head in those days, use to make people know the ____ man right away.

People were for and against the chin___ ____ first time my father chimb his head and cut his beard, wa____ ____ le did not know his age I think that he was older thar ____ ____ ho was forty-two years then.

When people hear he was going to c____ ____ tell him that he was going to ketch a cold ____ big argument among the older people. ____ up and shave up. My mother use to ____ bran. People use to think they ____ up. My father did get sick wi____ chimbing was the cause o____ years, he did not chimb ____ was one of the first ____ they had then to ____ gall the fingers, ____ nearly all m____ would l____ head ____ say. Some mothers would give the boys some shape of money when cutting the hair for the first time. And back then, it was a bit of celebration when a man was shaving his beard for the first time. Once upon a time, when some one become angry with a young fella, or if that young fella was troublesome, people would tell him that he will not live to shave his first beard. To live to shave the first beard means that the fella live to become a man.

Sometime in the early part of this century, some mothers take over the chimbing of their boys head. As time change when the mother chimb her son's head, people would call it "mother's touch". As the boys grow up, they resent the "mother's touch". They want the barber or a man to do the chimbing. "Mother's touch" come on the scene mainly because the family could not find the money to pay and the mother always have to do everything to the picknee. But still chimbing hair was far and few between. Our people would mostly have mind on where the next meal is coming from. The head and face full of hair was part and parcel of Estate life.

Haynes Smith was so determined that life in this land should change for the coming century that he stop the Clerk to Council from sleeping at the Court House. The Council was upstairs and the Court House was downstairs in the same building. After that he ~~ orders to clean and paint up the whole building. He then beg ~~ Country to send lawyers and officers to make the court

~~ to get out of the style of living in which
~~ was still rampant in the land so
~~ him. Haynes Smith take
~~ of the century
~~ ne. He

greatest gift the bakkra get from Haynes Smith, both for the ending of the century and the starting of the new one was a woman from Barbuda. They call her Lady Bethel but she say her name is Semarna, if I am calling it rightfully. She could hardly call her own name properly. She happen to attend to Bethel Codrington on his sick bed, during his final days, when she was a young young gal. The reason for her name, Lady Bethel she did not know. She did not know where she was born or even where she come from. She did not know where they were taking her when they move her from Barbuda to Antigua. She was a six footer with a broad face and a thick lip.

How Semarna or Lady Bethel get to this land, was that one of the biggest big shot bakkra of the land, John Tudway was not making any picknee. The Tudways owned Parham and Parham Plantation. That was close to 2,000 acres. Crawfords Plantation that people call Lodge also belong to them. Big people. The wife get to the point where she threaten to run-way. When big people wife run way in those days, that was a big shame. Whatever was the impediment, young Tudway could not see the way. He and his wife could not set horse[8] for that. But luck attend him. At the time a bakkra by the name of Massa Dougall own Lady Bethel. Dougall was a friend of Haynes Smith and Haynes Smith was the bosom friend of John Tudway and his wife Gretty. Haynes Smith know what Lady Bethel could do through Massa Dougall and he recommend that young John Tudway try she. Mark Tudway, father for John, and Governor Haynes Smith sail to Barbuda and get the woman to come to Antigua.

Lady Bethel start to work on young Tudway early o'clock. She turned the young man into a gineagag[9]. He start to make pick-nee after pick-nee. News spread, Barbuda woman a tickle-up lame Bakkra. Bakkra start to rush she down. She was forbidden to attend to any bakkra outside the big shot circle. I just get a glimpse

7. Not wanted.
8. Could not agree.
9. To become excessive in something.

of her when I was working at North Sound when I use to take Massa Hinds there. Me see how she rub and exercise the toes, the ankles, the shoulder blade and neck. She rub the centre and both sides of the head above the ears. She also rub around the navel and make circular rub around the heart. She warm her fingers over the lamp and hold Massa Hinds two ears. She also give him a mixture. The bakkra work she to death. She remain the only black person that they burry in Cockrum pond Burial Ground.

The plan to meet the new century was well on the way. The planters was into reparing or building new buff. The main talk was the future of sugar. Haynes Smith time run out before the century end.

At the turn of the century the planters plan many different activities to mark the time. The Anglican usually have one service on old year's night over the years. The planters use Big church for that. Old years night was a Big church night. But for the last day of the century every Anglican Church held its own service. All the services start at six in the afternoon. From the start up to ten was all singing and reading of the bible. Then the real service start at ten. Some time in the last hour, they fasten every door and window.

By then, who out keep out! All in dead stillness. Anything to wish or say was in the heart. At the stroke of mid-night, the bell start to toll and immediately they fling the doors and windows to greet the new century. The church bells ring for long while, the people sing and sing. My duty give me the chance to see Big church pack up with bakkra. All bakkra. I stay by the Goodwin house west of Government House until the service done. All the estates round the town ring their bells till dawn. Some estates people light fire at midnight in open plough fields to greet the dawn. The people make music of all kinds. And anyone can imagine the spree that follow with the bakkra and family.

The people of Sea View Farm say that no service could touch the one at Lebanon Moravian Church. According to them, Parson Christopher could not conduct a better service for the remainder of his days. He was deeply involved in the lives of his people. He got work for them. Doctor them when sick and keep them out of jail. His closing hymn was:

> *The sands of time are sinking,*
> *The dawn of heaven breaks,*
> *The summer morn I've sighed for,*
> *The fair sweet morn awakes.*

Just before the end of his sermon, the congregation sing out "O God, our help in ages past." The parson then break into an unusual hymn -

> *This, this is the God we adore,*
> *our faithful unchangeable friend.*

Just before the service done, he say to the youths. Go thou in life's fair morning, Go in the bloom of youth And buy for your adorning the precious pearl of truth. At the end of the service, he embrace everyone and tears flow from many in the congregation. After that large groups of people from the neighbouring villages would go to attend his old years night service. This was the main feature from that night until he became unable.

Haynes Smith successor, a governor they call F and F keep up one elaborate party. People claim that nearly all the planters get drunk and still they could not dry the barrel. While the planters get drunk and do other things to mark the end and the beginning of the centries, Nellie Robinson was doing something else. She was the busiest woman in the land. She help poor people close the century with thirty non-stop days of singing and Christmas concerts. She also keep up a big Thanksgiving Service for getting the strength from God to establish her Thomas Oliver Robinson High School in 1898 and for it to continue.

So that is how the century end. Lots of praying for better in the new century was done. People hope for better and for the new Governor to carry on the work of Haynes Smith.

Me live to see the New Governor F.&F did not have the guts to continue what Haynes Smith left behind. Under F. & F, the slums, the open kooka bendals, and deseases returned in full swing.

12
CHANGING TIMES:
Local teachers
took charge

Time was rolling on . The planters use to have their hands full, full to the brim with king sugar. When it was not the weather, it was the market, or the pests or plant disease. Sometimes all four problems hit the sugar industry, at the same time.

People know that the weather make you or break you. Too much rain can fall and spoil the sweet in the sugar. Too little rain can stunt the growth. But if the rain came in between you may have a good crop. The planters still face other big problems, at one time the biggest problem was pests and plant disease, both combine nearly end the sugar industry. In the 1880's, rats descended on the land like a plague. Ratta can't done!

They bit up field after field of sugar cane, Ratta nearly turn the massas crazy, poor people too have it hellish with them. They would bite anything and anybody. You couldn't leave a picknee unattended. The planters bring in a whole set of mongoose to kill the rats. Instead of paying attention to the rats, the mongoose turn to massa chicken.[1] All kinds of feather stock was on every estate.

The planters rush to protect the poultry. When mongoose get hungry, only so they turn on the rats. Mongoose against rats was not effective.

The mongoose still remain a mortal problem to the poultry industry. The planters put out a reward of one penny for every dead mongoose anyone would bring in. Just bring in the tail! Don't lug with the whole mongoose. A penny a tail spark off the building of mongoose traps all over the land. That was plenty money, a welcome relief for some of the hungry people.

Mongoose traps alone could not do enough to check the mongoose. Towards the end of the 1880's the planters become so scared over the mongoose threat to the feather stock that they allow poor people to own dogs to help track down mongoose. Before that, not a man could be drunk enough to live on the bakkra estate and own any dog. That animal was the security for massa only. Not nega people. The mongoose threat was so great to the important poultry industry that the planters have to ease the pressure and allow the nega-man to own dogs. Every dog own by the naga-man was to help ketch mongoose. Plenty wild dogs was in the land after a time. People use to search them out and borne[2] them. Antiguans then were not that kind to dogs because they always have in mind dogs were treated better than nega people.

The rats were not under control before in walk the insect they call the borer. This borer, bore up the sugar cane from the roots. The cane became hard-hard and produce far less juice. The sugar from it look like tar. People could neither eat the cane nor use the sugar with satisfaction. That was bad enough, but the most destructive thing to the sugar industry, in my time, was the disease they call the "rind fungus". That nearly close down king sugar for good. No joke, that nearly end the life of the King! In some of the fields the cane did not shoot up beyond two and three feet and the plant will only grow short joints.

---

1. Chicken here means all forms of poultry. Black people would use the phrase "mongoose eat chicken". Planters would talk about "mongoose eat poultry".
2. Stone.

At that time, the planters grow the sugar cane they call the Bourban variety. That variety was in use since sugar come to the land. The disease compel the planters to change them for harder types. This rind fungus put the planters on their knees. A special experiment station was set up at Friars Hill to help strengthen the other two at Skerritts and Bendals. Everything was done in order to stay on top of the situation. The Mother Country set up an Inquiry to find ways and means to save the sugar industry. That was the Norman Inquiry that take place in the 1890's. In those days when the Mother Country send people to inquire into something, the planters look towards that group to find hope. To restore hope in the sugar industry was the capital concern for the coming century.

One of the arguments of Governor Haynes Smith to the planters on the sugar industry, was that the small sugar mills in the land, will not stand up in the new century. He recommend that there should not be more than two large up to date sugar mills in the land. Most planters did not listen to him. After Haynes Smith left and the Norman Inquiry come, they also said the same thing. The planters decide to build one large sugar factory. All attention was on the building of this large new factory. Planters when they meet talk of the money they will get from it and how things would be done faster and better.

Except for the building and opening of the large Sugar Factory at Gunthropes in 1902 to 1905, nothing tangible happen to make the early start of the 1900's better for the poor people. Between 1900 and 1906 four governors sit in Government house. That period was somewhat unsettling. Some massass get fed up of the land and did not allow the new century to meet them in it. In that same period, some of the old guards dead out and new ones take charge.

The big names of the new century were mostly those that have connections with the building and operating of the new central sugar factory. George Moody-Stuart was the biggest name after the governor. Then there was a G. Watt and the Henckel DuBuisson family. In 1902, the planters put up a new building near

Government house for the rich and powerful bakkra. No woman could cross foot there. New century, new place to spree. They name it New Club. It was around that same period that estate owners begin to scrap their jail one by one and all prisoners have to serve their time at the big jail in town. In the early 1890's Haynes Smith did tell the planters to scrap the estate dungeons and make one jail, but they did not listen. At the time, Sour Betty, the name of Betty's Hope Jail was the largest and one of the first to close. Parsons Maules jail, the Torturer, close after Master Edwards pass on in 1907. That was the year before my wife had her first-born. Long Lane estate jail go on the longest. That closed only after Willie Moore break out and go bout his business. That was in 1920 or there about.

Prisoners have to work all over the island mostly in the quarry, on the roads and in the fields. They build jail houses on wheels to serve that purpose. A prison gang will leave the big jail on Mondays and return on Saturdays. The big jail was the jail for the Leeward Islands since the 1870's. It did not serve the purpose properly until after the turn of the century. The other Islands' prisoners would have to get a year or more in jail to warrant the transportation to the main jail in Antigua.

Another thing that take place during the early years of the century, was that the Goodwins send me to cart a whole pile of books to the Big Court in St. John's. The massas hold a picnic for the man that sail from the Mother Country to come to fix up the Big Court. So early a'clock in the new century they put in place the Big jail and the Big court.

All eyes were on the new Gunthrope sugar factory to help with plenty work. But because the estates turn their grinding over to the central factory, many more people were put out of work at the very start of the new century than at anytime during the last one. Bear this in mind, after the people was back on the plantation, the need for the Portuguese labour vanish with speed.

Some Portuguese start their own business. In quick time, the

Portuguese spread their wings all over. Antonio Camacho, one-time groom at Long Lane Estate, was one of the first to begin to buy and sell things. In no time at all, he start to buy land. He buy the seaside land near Redcliffe Street. His family then make attempt to buy out Jackass Point, another seaside land. The English massas say woe-dey, no more seaside land in this city for Portuguese. The English massa then stop them from going on the estates to sell goods. That further check their speed. At one time some of the English bakkra make this rule: "Buy from the Portuguese, go live and work with the Portuguese". The pressure slow the Portuguese down but only for a while. A couldn't tell a soul where the Portuguese get money from but as soon as any estate was up for sale, they would be right there ready to buy them up. That puzzle the English Massas. The Camacho family take over Blakes Estate form Henry Elliot. The same Camacho family went on to buy Briggins, Brooks, Mount Pleasant, Millers and Stony Hill. Another Portuguese group led by the De Souza family take over Parsons Maules and Barnacle Point. Up to then, the nega-man did not have a copper. Our lot was to shoot the hard labour for the massas.

It was right for the Portuguese to do business even though they would get some trouble from the English massas. The sad thing was neither the Portuguese nor the English massas want the ex-slaves nor their picknee to live by themself nor do what business they choose.

A man by the name of Jack Lard occupy an old estate house that was left ruin near Ottos Estate.

Not a man trouble him until he start to buy and sell things in the old house. A Portuguese man they call Mark Barretto burn him out. Joe Knight, another ex-slave picknee, start to sell subbon at English Harbour and the English bakkra from that side flatten the place with fire. And so it was, our place was back on the estate to shoot hard labour.

Nellie Robinson use to preach over and over again that people who will not learn to read will not be able to get good jobs at the new sugar factory and they won't be able to run their own business. That stir some people. She decide whosoever will may come, be they bastard[3] or wedlock to she school. That throw the fat in the fire. Bastard in Secondary School! Can't happen. The Anglican Plantocrats refuse to recognize her school. In those days woman usually bow down to man. Nellie Robinson bow not to priest nor to the powerful Anglican bishop. She was a woman and a half! She just move on and left the mighty priests and planters behind. She continue to take in bastards and also to cover the land with a series of concerts year after year.

Some hope for nega people start to come a little before the start of the 1914- 18 war or there about. Up come a batch of teachers from the ex-slaves picknee at that period. That was the batch that start to replace the priests and parsons that have been doing the little teaching since the freedom.

There was another batch that get into nursing about the same time. They gradually replace the english midwife. To some local people the event that make a big impact on the people was that period when local teachers came on the scene. Say after me, up to now no one surpass them early teachers. They give their all. The Mother Country take over the responsibility of the running of the school three or four years before the start of World War 1914- 18.

The first Inspector of schools come to the land in 1912 and none come back until after the war.

The inspector use to come in June and examine the whole school all together. That was in the reading, reciting and singing in the open hall. Ricmatic was by itself. Back then the Inspector was very special on discipline. Just barely look back, out of the class that pupil would have to go. Some pickenega, particularly boys, when they did not feel too sure of themself would deliberately look back to get the "drive out order"[4]. If anyone was lucky enough to escape the drive out order for not paying proper attention, that pupil would

3. In Antigua at that time children born out of wedlock were not allowed to attend Secondary Schools.

not escape it if it happens when singing "God Save The King"or
"God Save the Queen". My own picknee Wally, always get the
"drive out" order and he take it make joke.

The teaching process was slow, slow what you call slow, but
more and more young people particularly from the town were learning to read. They use to show off on country people. Me think that
the Seven Standard exam start after the 1914- 18 war. In those days
teachers surely did not spare the rod and spoil the picknee. That
keep some pickeenega out of school. But no one can doubt that the
rod help bring them up in a respectful way. They couldn't drunk do
the things I see them doing today. Back side would pay. Pickeenega
back then, have plenty manners for their teachers, priests, police and
older heads. Sometimes I now have to wonder which of these people get the least respect nowadays. Pickeenega don't count them
tall-tall now. They rude to everybody , they pass old people like they
all sleep in the same house. Days gone by[5] they would get blow from
that old man or woman and more from the mother when she hear.
Not such thing now.

As time change the Nellie Robinson teaching ketch on.
Some people want their picknee to get good work at the factory and
they start to suck sall and drink water to give them a little learning.
As usual, plenty picknee was the go then. The first set could not see
a school door. It was mostly the younger ones that get to go to
school from the parents that could afford it.

The reading and reciting and singing was the go. Schools use
to hold plenty concerts. I cannot stop thinking of Christmas after
the turn of the century when the schools and other groups from the
villages did have the reciting, the singing and the acting of plays. All
that and the singing round use to make people don't want the
Christmas season to end. I think that the Nellie Robinson teaching
start to bear fruit.

4. School children were expected to stand at attention when singing the
   English national anthem or would be driven out the school.
5. Less respect is given today to people in Authority but in early days children
   would be punished for disrespecting older people, teachers and priests.

171

People have it to say that one of the first product from the Nellie Robinson High School was Joe Blake a man from the town. He become second man at Public Works after a while. As soon as Blake come Boss-man he get a long pipe, walk with his hands cock out from his side and he would kimbo them just like the bakkra and he would puff his pipe and make his own brother see living hell. His pass words was "We de whites don't make jokes". Anything he had to say, he would begin with "We de whites" and the people call him "We de Whites". And let me tell you the man face just little bit lighter than mine! Some shelterless people use to sleep in the horse stable at Public Works. He would drive them out ever so often. The painful thing was that he would only drive them out when rain set up or if it was falling because he know that they did not have any place to go. The bakkra never drive them out yet in the rain! One minute late for work and Blake would take out a hunk of money out of their pay. His own people cry out gainst he. And the more they cry the worse he behave. Anyway, one day, just suddenly, the Public Works massa tell him not to come back. People knock tin pan and dance in the street. Happy, them happy so! Charlie Cockram was another one. He only get a little power at the Board of Health. He too was from Nellie Robinson High School. Immediately, he order that no food cooking on the job. Workers were accustomed to cook at lunch time. If time over run them he would go and out down[6] the fire, throw way the food and force them to work on hungry belly. And don't quarrel! Up, he will send them for licks and on top of that, money hunk out of pay. He use to tell the workers, "Look, when me done lie pan ar-you, not a man can escape the blazing of his back". The behavior of those early set of bosses from our own people nearly kill me. They really have me going. Me grow to fraid them bad, bad, bad. And it was in every corner. Shadow cast over the hope that many people had. The thing is they should get off them high horses, but they think they were right. My own villager Alfred Mack was another one, that he use to go to Nelly Robinson Night Class. Mack mother use to keep a bakkra call Bobby Hughes.

Bobby was a big man[7] at the jail. He pull a string[8] for Mack and Mack become one of the first black jail officer in the land. Few people then, could ever dream that the time would come when ex-slave picknee would get big job at the big jail. If nothing else that kind of work was only for the massas. The time did come and to me that was capital of all the changes up to then. A wonder if you would understand me when I say that Mack come bakkra right away. He start to go church at the Freeman's Village Methodist Church - hand full with books, arms swinging and chest and belly push out with pocket watch pin cross from shoulder to side pocket. He would deliberately go church late and walk right through the service from back to front. Won't take off his planter hat until he find a seat. After he find the seat, he look round and then kneel down briefly, then sit up. God alone know if he pray or not! Mack became showie-showie like a man monkey. Too big for the village with that he leave Freeman's Village Methodist Church and join the Anglican church at All Saints. There he become mortally edge-up with some bakkra and particularly with the Goodwin family that live at Duers and U-mans Estate. After a time, there was not a jail man that happen to be under the control of Mack that did not have subbon gainst he. Matters get worse after they promote Mack to use the cat-o-nine. Big subbon! Mack come catter for jail! When Mack happen to come home in the village or go to church on Sundays, he usually find a crowd and would brag again and again, how every jail man 'fraid he. He was a loud mouth. He brag and say, 'When me trow the cat 'cross them back, it would be a good time before them ketch themself'. He talk of a prison rule where prisoners must be blind folded before they cat them. That was to protect the catter and family from jailman vengeance. But Mack brag to the village people how he don't follow that rule. He love when they feel he hand and see he face when he drive lash under them backside. "Manners them with the cat across them back. Lickrich if them come back!" Mack would boast and would end up saying no body can do me nutton.

7 A man that wheel his authority at the prison.
8 A form of nepatism.

"Me na fraid them."

Mack half brother, Neville serve time in jail for breaking cane. One day after eating, Neville throw the eating pan into the wash-dish. Mack say that he throw the pan too hard. That was disrespect to the Crown. He put on seven days on to the time of his blood brother. Neville family and friends meet Mack and trouble he 'bout wa he do[10] Neville. Mack mek[11] big noise in the road. He cuss them and some of what he tell them was, "When one man dey a jail - a jail ee day - fu larn manners-[12] and when they slip out a line put more manners under them tail don't mine who the person, put them back in line!"

Tranie, another Freeman Village man serve a jail term for wounding Bucksie. Tranie tell the village people that Mack make him swallow a half penny. Mack suspect that Tranie was up to something and call search. Mack squeeze up Tranie mouth, look down his throat and hit him at the back of his head. Tranie say it was a good thing he actually swallow the money before he get the blow behind his head because the thing pass his throat hole so slow that he become frighten, wondering if it would stick. But say me Sammy say, every hallelujah have the Amen[13] with it. Don't mind how long it take to come. Sometimes it come real sudden. At other times, it may delay for a while. When people haven't the least thought the Amen come. Mack Prison gang was at Liberta fixing the village road and he fall in love with a woman from neighbouring Falmouth. After he lock up the jail men at nights in the jail house, he would go to Falmouth to look for his newly found sweetheart. A man they call Draggy from English Harbour was a prisoner in the gang. Mack give Draggy six with the cat because Draggy did not stand at attention when Mack was talking to the prisoners one morning. All of a sudden, Mack start to nice up with Draggy

9. The person responsible for the beating of prisoners.
10. Question his motives.
11. Make.
12. As far as Mack was concerned jail was to reform the thinking of prisoners.
13. A belief that all things will come to an end.

along with the other prisoners, even though he would still hammer them to the ground so often. Mack never hesitate to use the catonine for the least thing and add time on them. Anyway, some friend for Draggy pinch Draggy and tell him that them officer left them up at nights and go to sleep with his woman at Falmouth and he and she go dancing regularly at the Picadilly Dance House.

Draggy tell the rest what he hear and they plan for Mack. One night, when Mack and his woman was on their spree, out break the jail men in the pitch of night. All of them buss out and go brok[14] Zandy Shop in Liberta. They clean up Zandy bread and saltfish. When them done eat all they want, they start to sing. The noise wake up the village. People find out that jail man had feast at Zandy Shop. People nearly have fit when they find out it was jail men that cut loose. The bigger the crowd get, the more they sing and dance. Police surround the place. Jailman refuse to move! They say, "Mack must come!" When Mack reach to start the day, not a prisoner in the jail house. Mack nearly drop dead - frighten, wonder what is going on! Then he hear that his gang brok Zandy Shop and were waiting for him[15]. And they were also singing and dancing too! He shout "murder, oh me belly." Mack rush with bird speed to Zandy Shop. When he reach at the shop and see what happen he bawl out and say "Oh gad! Me belly! Wha mek ar-you do me that?" Draggy shout out viciously at him and say "anybody that play good bad, this a wha them fu get". Then Draggy hoist up his shirt and show the crowd how Mack wail up[16] his back for nothing. Up to the time Mack reach, jail man refuse to move. They continue them singing and dancing and say Massa Noble have to come.

Noble was the over all man for the prison. He arrive later and take charge and send home Mack.

14. To break and enter.
15. To wait for.
16. Scars resulted from severe beating.

The Governor hold an investigation into the break out. The revelation was that Mack left up the jail house night after night, over a long period of time. They also find out that from time to time, when he was leaving up the jailmen to themself, he would call a few of them by name and when he get no answer, he would believe that they were asleep. He would then slip away on his journey. The jailmen tell the investigators that, they use to answer if they were not sleeping, but when they plan for him that night, they did not answer and Mack think they were asleep and when he gone them do for him. The incident with Mack bring an immediate end to mobile prisons in Antigua. The prison head add one month on the time of each prisoner and compensate Zandy for his loss because the loss was due to deliberate negligence of the servant. Then they throw Mack off his high horse. Draggy, who was serving time for stealing a pig, tell the investigator that he could spend the balance of his life in jail now he see the fall of Mack the Satan from his high horse. And a tell you that was a heavy fall. When Mack was riding the high horse, Freeman's Village Methodist Church was too poor for him.

But after he get the fall[17], back to Freeman's Village Methodist Church he start come again. And believe it or not, he want people to sorry for him. At first, he was like a leper. Then he gradually crawl back to some of the very people that he did not want to see.

Not all Antiguans are like Mack. In the late thirties there was a young man call Sydney Christian, a Lawyer. Some planters use to refer to him as the double edge razor. According to them, old Sydney Christian could do law any part in the Empire as well as any part in 'Merica. He come Merican lawyer before the Empire. He pass first in Merica, then he go from Merica to England and pass up again. The planters them say he win a big murder case in St.

17. Revenge

Thomas just before the 1939 World War broke out. Big crowd use to go to hear him argue in town. At one time the people in court clap him after he done talk and the judge drive out all a dem. Later on, Old Sydney just roll his tongue to the judge for them and the judge allowed them back in the courtroom. After the case done, he got such a clapping, that people all round the street come to find out what was happening.

When Old Sydney was on his way home from England, the ship get stranded off the sea at Martinique and was forced to dock in Martinoque. The lady Nelson bring home the Leward Islands passengers. Old Sydney make a lot of planter friends and according to planter Winter, he tell them that his journey from England to Antigua was far more exciting than his journey from Merica to England. The Lady Nelson pull in at all the Leward Islands before coming to Antigua. He make sure he touch down on all of them and he long want to make that mark. I use to feel very proud of Old Sydney perhaps he was the first Antiguan to make a mark to be able to practice law any part of the English world and that was telling me that black people were going places.

As the years roll more and more of the neglected people get a hold where the planters never dream they would. The top jobs at the sugar factory was the hardest to break into. I learn though that changes will always take place through man and providence, don't mind how hard life may seem to be. And so despite those who get on high horses, many local teachers provided grounds for a better life. I comfort myself with the belief that everybody will not get on the high horse. Don't mind how bad the situation may be, take it from me, while there is life, there's hope. The number now that can read and write and can do things properly is more than a few that feel the world belongs to them. From what I pass through I can say that man will always abuse authority. So too there will be those who will always cry against abuse. I always think that much more

good people are in the world than rotten ones and they will sweat
hard to make it better in the face of greed, abuse, and hardship.

13
POWERFUL FORCES AT WORK: Judicial Power and Obeah Culture

One of the kind of work that some nega man fit into rapidly at the turn of the century was to be a Local Constable. They replace the bakkra who use to do that kind of work. As in the bakkra time, a local constable could arrest you and hall you before the Magistrate. They carry a thing call a shackle[1] a club-stick and sometimes a dog to assist them.

The local constable abuse their power to the proper. Believe it or not, I cannot remember, one time when anybody say that they give their people a break if they do wrong. In all our ups and downs, in all the hunger we bear and with all the forces that force our people to steal, and do bad things, I don't remember, not one time, when our own local Constable ease up on the poor people. The bakkra could depend on them to keep the jail full with their own kind. Very often, it would be false oath they give that send their own to the work house.[2] Back then, anything the Constables say was the bible truth[3] for the bakkra and the Magistrates. From what I can remember, only one Magistrate after quite a while,

1. Handcuffs
2. Jail

Robert Batkin, that would put the local Constable on the spot and question their complaint. That was a big change, almost unbelievble. Batkin was the planter enemy. Some people say Robert Batkin was half Irish and half Scottish.

Watchman[4] was active on the estates guarding the sugar cane. Always on the look out for people stealing anything but braking sugar cane in particular. Watchman Assy Calbourne carry up[5] a man call Plunto to Massa Affie Goodwin for breaking cane. During the argument, Plunto took a piece of wood and knock Assy out cold and scamper out of sight. Not a man could find Plunto. They search all over until them weary.

Years after this incident Plunto was seen in Mingo[6] cutting cane on a plantation. He tell them that he ketch a ride on the Dye Wood Boat[7] to Mingo because he believe he kill Assy. Assy was not dead, but was unconscious for weeks. The blow turn him trupit[8] He never did watch man work again.

Another man that I know run from trouble and escape on the Dye Wood Boat was a man call Nyampas from Cotton Estate. He killed his sweetheart Missy Crighton of All Saints, and then cattch a ride on the Dye Wood boat and sink[9] the land. He left a lasting joke and a big lesson for the people and the police. Nyampas take off his clothes and quietly leave them at the edge of Cotton Estate pond. When Cotton nega house people saw the clothes, they say them belong to Nyampas. Everybody say the same thing Nyampas drown himself. Big news broke. Large crowd gather round pond side. Horse guard the police and the Magistrate show

3. To swear under oath.
4. A security guard.
5. To actually take him up to the Massa to answer for his actions.
6. Santo Domingo.
7. The Dye Wood Boat was so named because it transported logwood, that made dye.
8. Stupid.
9. Leaves the country.

up. Then divers came and dive out the pond searching for Nyampas body. No body come up. People set to work and bale the water out of the pond. No Nyampas body up to then. People who know Nyampas hold onto them bible oath that the clothes belong to him. Search call off. People call the pond Nyampas Pond up to this day.

Police and other people keep looking out for Nyampas. Then come the big rumour all over the place, that a Dab Dab, a big obeah man from Potters Village get way Nyampas out of the land. Smart obeah man Dab Dab did not miss the opportunity. He claim that he make people see Nyampas and take him for somebody else. Dab Dab crow and crow[10] that Nyampas did not run or hide.[11] Nyampas he also claim, settle up all his business with his family and friends and then leave the land. Wash tun a people believe Dab Dab. I mean plenty people believe him.

Dab Dab was not a man that keep still. He always ride his donkey to town to show off. In town he never tie his donkey. He usually put his walking stick in front on the ground close to the donkey two front foot. After that he would go where he like. Stop as long as he like, and the donkey never move. He feed the donkey with whatever he eat, bread, crackers, roast dumpling, fungi, potato, yam, anything. When Dab Dab put his hand in fusie, the donkey lick off his hand clean, clean clean. Sometimes he would put some of the fusie on his head and the donkey would lick off Dab Dab head clean of the fusie. That was a sight.

People who happen to be in the city when Dab Dab was around flock to see him and his donkey perform. The biggest thing of the day was when Dab Dab was ready to get on the donkey back. He would only say lea-go and donkey would stoop down and Master Dab Dab jump on his donkey back and donkey would move on. That was the advertisement. So when the rumour started that a Dab Dab get way Nyampas, that was it. Name spread like wildfire. Dab Dab, Potter super obeah man have the rush. People from all over would flock just to catch a glimpse of the biggest obeah man

10. Talk frequently about the same thing.
11. Nyampas simply leave the land in his own time.

of the land. Early o'clock in the new century, the bakkra pass law to beat anyone they catch working obeah when they enter jail and when they were leaving jail.

Jackass say the world na label. Not a police, nor local constable, nor bakkra, not a man take Dab Dub before any magistrate. Don't mind how cross them bakkra be against obeah. Dab Dab free to do what he want, not a man touch him. Only Magistrate Batkin would ask why no one ever bring the re-noun Dab Dab before any Magistrate. Sometime ago a local constable, name Roy Mann of Sanderson Estate carry up coffee woman, Lucy Myers to the Magistrate. He tell the magistrate that he ketch her working obeah. The Magistrate happen to be Batkin. Much to the dislike of the Sanderson bakkra, Massa Noel, after Batkin hear the constable explain the case, he ask him if he know Dab Dab. Constable Roy Mann tell the Magistrate yes. Batkin in a rage dismiss the case and drive the constable from before him. You See, the constable would never touch an obeah man from Potters, because at that time everybody was afraid of Potter people.

Not so long after, there was the sho-sho,[13] Nyampas was in Mingo. Then people that happen to come back from Mingo, bring news that Nyampas really was there. Cyril Bago a friend of mine and cousin to Nyampas dead sweetheart Missy Crighton, travel to Mingo to cut cane, and meet up with Nyampas. When he come back he tell All Saints people that he and Nyampas cut cane side by side in Mingo and he tell Nyampas that he hear he kill Missy Crighton and Potter biggest obeah man get him out the land.

Bago say that Nyampas tell him when he realise a dead the woman dead, he go to Cotton Estate pond side, leave his dirty clothes right beside the pond because he know people would believe that he drown himself. Cotton people know the hat he wear if nothing else. While they were diving him out, he would look how best to sink the land. Cyril Bago say that Nyampas say that he was just lucky to catch the Dyewood boat that was sailing out at the time.

12. To actually take him up to the Massa to answer for his actions.
13. Rumour.

Nyampas say it was not a plan but plain luck that attend him. It was a love quarrel that get him in the trouble. According to Bago, Nyampas tell him that he could not tell a soul how Dab Dab look.

I live long with some powerful men and women on this earth. If man and woman were created little lower than angel they, can be little lower than the devil also. No body could steal from Baxy Washer of my village and don't get caught. Go in his ground and see if you could get out without he take you out. Where he get the power from, God Almighty know. All what happen I think in this particular case is that Dab Dab was not a fool. He quickly use the Nyampas escape to fool some people and get some ready money out of them.

Every now and then, the name of a big obeah-man would spring up in the land. There was a Professor Daniel from Dominica. People use to say that he could turn himself invisible. He did not go back to Dominica after serving a jail term in Antigua. The big rumour was that when he was to be in jail, people would see him out and around and by the time the guards miss him and ask for him, he would be in the cell. The other saying, was whenever they lash him, the Governor wife use to feel the licks and so the authorities have to stop beating him. Next thing, it was like wildfire that Professor Daniel was good at finding jumbie money.

Once upon a time, there was the belief that money was hidden under the earth all over the place. And wherever any money was, the older heads say that a jumbie would be sure to be there guarding the money. The jumbie usually dream some family member or friend and tell them about the money. The Menzes family of Swetes claim that some pass generation for them dream them and tell them where to dig to get some money. They went with speed and dig and dig but no money come up. At last, they decide to get Professor Daniel to dig up the money for them. Everything was set for the professor to dig up this money. The Menzes family anxious, can't keep them heel, want the money bad.

Some time pass, and man, they neither see nor hear from proffessor Daniel. Worst of all the jumbie stop dreaming them and the Menzes start to worry. They then get the feeling that the Professor take up the money behind their backs, and with that, they reported him to the police. Big subbon! Police lock up the Professor and charge him for concealing jumbie money. When the news break nearly every mortal in this land believe that the professor take up the money behind the Mendes back.

On the day of the court setting, the courtroom was packed with people from all over, and so was the street outside of the court-house. Nearly the whole of Swetes Village come to hear the big and unusual case and to get a glimpse of the Professor.

The Professor brought his mother from Dominica to give evidence for him. She tell Magistrate Dyett that her son is not a pauper and would not conceal any money. Dyett tell her that the more some man have, the more they want, and that he was not convinced that the professor was all that innocent. However, in the end the magistrate dismissed the case and there was the uproar. Noise from all corners. Some say good the most say bad. Sammy Martin from Freeman's Village, mouth like bell! Man, he drown out everybody. He say that no magistrate should listen to such trupidness. Sammy nyam fire in every crowd, "There is no such thing call obeah" "None obeah dey" and he know that the magistrae would have to let go the Professor. Sammy did not remember that the good book say, that 'be sure your sins will find you out.'

Well, the same Sammy use to work with a man name Blair of Freeman Village. One Sunday, he carry back Blair horse without the saddle. When do stop, it was coffee woman Neptune from Winthrope that huff[14] the saddle because Sammy won't pay for work she do for him. Sammy bawl and tell she that he neither own horse nor saddle. That did not shake coffee woman Neptune. She held fast to the saddle.

Sammy had to go back to Freeman's Village without the sad-

14. The Coffee woman hold onto the saddle in exhange for work done for Sammy.

dle. He tell Blair that a woman name Madam Neptune huff the saddle just because he owe she for some food. Sammy beg Blair to lend him the money. Blair say, not my money. Sammy try all he know to get the money to prevent Blair from going for the saddle. All Blair had in mind was that he did not know this woman from Adam and he want his saddle back. Blair ready to journey to Winthrope to look about his saddle, but Sammy just won't go with Blair all he want was some one to help him out with the money. After some haggling Sammy decided to go with Blair to Winthrope to see the woman. When Sammy and Blair reached Winthrope, Blair couldn't sing sweet enough to coffee woman Neptune. She tell Blair, day in day out she do everything that Sammy want. Sammy say she work good but he just won't pay. Madam Neptune keep her word "no money, no saddle". The coffee woman mean that from head to foot. Blair was taken back. Sammy did not tell him the real truth why the woman hold on to the saddle. Blair could not ride without his saddle. He eventually pay the woman the money. The coffee woman start to sell herself to Blair. She want to show that she did not rob Sammy nor hard with him. From one argument to the next, she open she note book and show Blair all what she do for Sammy. What a thing! Fat trow way in de fire![15] Blair see his own name in the Book. He nearly dead! Sammy ask coffee woman Neptune to driff[16] everybody from around Blair because he want all the work. Blair could not catch himself. He attack Sammy right there and Sammy left Winthrope with bird-speed. When Blair reach back to Freeman's Village, he 'larm up the place and Sammy take Blair and make him mortal enemy. Blair tell the village people that when he see his name in the coffee woman book he bawl like a likkle picknee. After that, anytime Sammy get sick, he tell people that Blair and coffee woman Neptune set folks on him. The name "Folks" stick on Sammy to this day. Blair could call the police and mash up the subbon, but he keep it down. The way those bakkra use to punish people over this obeah story cause suffering for guilty

15. Big controversy between Blair and Sammy increases.
16. To use her mystical powers to rid Blair of the people that sourrounded him.

185

and innocent. Some people that have malice 'gainst their neighbour use to make false oath 'gainst them saying they see them working obeah. The bakkra would not wait to know if it was true or false. Away with them before the magistrate. No use doubt. Jail for sure and back wale up until death.

Right in this same village, Freddy Dubang and Manny Emanuel spend time in work house, because Marty Hope say they work obeah upon she. Marty Hope show the police where she claim that she see them plant the bottle. Police pluck up the bottle planted in the yard. The police then lock up Dubang and Manny. Magistrate Dyette give them three months a piece, with twelve strokes on the day they enter and twelve on the day they let them out. On his way to jail Dubang cried out saying "Oh to me God, me want Batkin to try me." When Dubang come out of jail he make a benna on the whole jail term. He sing how much them bang him in and out of jail and nearly kill him for what he never do. Part of the benna go like this:

> Dem bang me in, Dem bang me out,
> Dem nearly kill me.
> Not me, a-na me, me neighbour lie pon me.
> She lie pon me woe, woe, she lie pon ar-we
> Not me Duban, not he Manny
> The bitch lie pon ar-we
> Batkin, Oh Lord, Batkin
> Batkin would a hear ar-we.

Not long after the jail term Marty Hope got sick. She lay in her dying bed and start to call list.[17] She call Dubang and Manny and beg them pardon. She confess how she lied on them and that they suffer innocent jail. She also confess she burried the bottle herself and she wanted to put Dubang in jail but Manny was his best friend so she decided to rope in both. The only reason why she set

17. A death bed confession.

them up is because Dubang has a daughter that wear shoes before her daughter. The confession larm[18] up the village. Duban mother cry and cry and curse and curse but the damage was done. Marty Hope passed on leaving bitterness and hatread behind.

A lady that people call Mama Silly and another woman name Clarry, again they come from Freemans Village. I have to say that my village people were not the worst in the land. The people will always remember that the same cry at Moroe was always the same cry at Briggins. Mama Silly and Clarry always have some niff-ishness over a man name George Bournes. Bournes was a stock overseer at North Sound. Both women love the man and so both hate one another to death. Clarry want to get rid of Mama Silly before Mama Silly get rid of her. Clarry try the same thing that Marty do to Dubang and Manny. Clarry report to the police that she and Constable Martin ketch Mama Silly burying a bottle in her yard. Police go and find the bottle with liquid. He lock up Mama Silly and charge she for working obeah on Clarry.

On the day of the setting, as soon as local Constable Martin start to explain to Magistrate Batkin about what he see Mama Silly do, Mamma Silly grab him and hit him two slap in his face and hold on tight on Martin and would not let him go.

Police spring pon she. Magistrate Richard Batkin order her arrest and adjourn the setting in the midst of the commotion. In those days, the person who make the complaint and the one who have to answer along with the witness were all on the same stand at the same time. After the commotion cool down the setting resume and police separate them. Court full. Crowd run over in the streets. Not a chance they take. The police shackle Mama Silly.

The magistrate tell Mama Silly that she is a devil and that he never read nor witness before what she do. The magistrate ask her to explain why she do what she had done. Mama Silly look straight at the magistrate and tell him, "Massa, you can lock from a tief, but not from a dam liar". Every man in court mouth wide open, can't

18. The talk of all the village people.

believe what they hear. Mama Silly then turn to local constable Martin and say, "Martin, look in me face. You know you lie. You know a one set-up between you and Clarry for me to go jail and get blow in and out." Magistrate Batkin properly put his tongue on Mama Silly, and then dismiss the obeah charges. To the big surprise of everybody, Magistrate Batkin bound her over to keep the peace for some months. People could not believe that Mama Silly did not get a day in jail. The big argument of the land was how could somebody slap down a witness in court-a local constable and did not get a day in jail. And the thing was Mama Silly did not show one drop of penitence.

Although there would be some Coffee Women who can do things, a good number of them that profess they can work obeah always find somebody to put out of the way. I am not on the coffee women back more than anybody else. Quack in everything, even among some of them that run up and down pulpit. Coffee woman Magee say that she get off Mama Silly but Mama Silly disown she. Back then there was a big joke on Jacob Tittle of Freeman's Village. He badly want a job at the sugar factory. So he decided to go to one big time coffee woman at Potters to make him get the job. He find one they call Norma Pelle. Coffee woman Pelle give Jacob some powder and tell him to rub up with it whenever he decided to go about the job hunting. Madam Pelle also beg Jacob hard, not to talk to anybody when he set out from his home and he must not look back before he talk to the manager about the job. She charge Jacob one shilling and tell him to go about the job the coming Monday. Road usually full on Monday mornings with people going to look work. Loads of people always flock at Factory gate mostly on Monday mornings looking for work.

Anyway, this Monday morning, Jacob rub up with the powder. Neck and face white. Jacob set his face straight. Don't mind who hail up Jacob, he would see and don't see. Hear and don't hear. Some people think that he was getting off his head. And more so because his face look whitish. Jacob reach Factory early and stand right in front of the gate. Ignoring any hello, and with face straight with the gate. Claxton, a bosom friend of Jacob, was on the same mission and meet Jacob at the gate. He greet Jacob. Jacob did not answer. He look at Jacob and get the feeling that he may have some problems. So he hold Jacob and tell him all of us have it hard and he must not rest problems on his mind. Pray and God will help you. It was the kind of situation that force Jacob to talk to his long time friend. Naturally he broke Coffee Woman order. Picking time come and the Manager did not pick Jacob. Claxton get pick, to report next day for work. Jacob was blue mad. He blame Claxton. He tell Claxton right outside the gate that it was he Claxton that bring bad luck on him and make the job come out his hands.

Claxton could not fathom why Jacob throw blame on him. According to Claxton he was worried and he never rest until he get out of Jacob the reason for the blame. When Claxton hear Jacob reason, he nearly dead with laugh. Jacob was deadly serious and insist that it was Claxton that interfere with him that cause the bad luck that day. And he done with Claxton.

Claxton could not keep what Jacob tell him. Tory jump out[19] in the crowd and it was a big laugh. The same people call to mind how Jacob was operating and walking as if he has a stiff neck. Claxton tell Jacob to pray to Almighty God for help. Jacob had no Almighty God to pray to. He went back to the Coffee Woman. Potter village coffee Woman Pelle know that she gave Jacob an almost impossible task. Before Jacob could open his mouth she tell him that a disobedient man will loose out more than a disobedient picknee and she have no time to waste with people who do not follow instruction. Jacob had no shame. He tell the village people that Claxton make coffee woman Pelle vex with him. The Jacob joke was a big one for a long time. People began act like him. They would white up their faces, walk straight and would mock Jacob world without end. Some people use to act a play they call the Jacob

---

19. Every body get to know the seceret.

Play.

Coffee Woman Norma Pelle get into trouble not too long after the Jacob story. Police lock her up for working obeah. She own it up to Magistrate Batkin and Batkin let her off. That was not heard of before. I don't think that a bakkra could be found in this land who was not mortified with Batkin when they hear the news. Batkin was not afraid of them and listen to this one.

Old Elizabeth from Duers Estate, steal Massa Brooks cock fowl. She would have a good supper with that.

Somebody chat pon she. Police lock her up and charge her with stealing the cock fowl. Nega don't miss jail when they steal, much less when they steal bakkra subbon. On the day of the setting, she tell Magistrate Batkin that a hungry make she take the cock and make soup. Batkin say he know what hungry can make people do. He warn her and let she go. Big uproar! All the bakkra got on Batkin back. Batkin must not be magistrate any longer. The Goodwins that I work for, was vex with Batkin to the proper, and they talk off Batkin behind his back. They say that Batkin was not a true English man even though he was born in England. His mother was Scottish and his father Irish. The Governor will have to give him another position because Batkin don't understand one thing about the work of a magistrate.

I think that Massa George Goodwin was closer to Batkin than most people. Close is what people would call High-ti-tie-ti friends. Some long time after he set the Elizabeth case, watchman Mason ketch Hepp from Burks Estate red handed in a field belonging to George Goodwin, eating cane and have some cut up in her bag. The Goodwins do everything to prevent Batkin to have anything to do with the case. In the end, they had to give way because Magistrate Dyett dock out of the case.

They ill-treat the woman and march she up to Batkin. The setting take place at Burks Estate court house. The place pack with bakkra from all over as if they could frighten Batkin.

Hepp tell the magistrate that she was guilty and that she

make up her mind to serve the time because not even one copper she have to call her own. I was not in court. I have to stay with the horse and cart outside. But I hear Batkin was cool and the amount of bakkra present did not shake him. He told the court that when they make him magistrate and at the same time decide to send all prisoners to the central prison, he decide in his own mind that he will not send any woman to a prison where male and female prisoners have to walk through the same gate. That he believe that a woman should not be put behind bars unless she committ a violent crime. And further, said Magistrate Batkin, no ordinary man should be in charge of a jail where woman prisoners are held. The Church of England would have to be in command of the jail and the priest to be in charge of the operation before he send any woman to spend time. The priests he said are the best to change lives. After the magistrate done talk his piece, he told Hepp to get piece of land to work and grow her own cane and food. He bound her over for six months and let her go. Hepp tell Magistrate Batkin thanks while water gush from her eyes.

Hepp was not too far from court when Bobby Williams, George Goodwin's groom grab her and start to fight her. Hepp daughter join in the fight and the horse guard part the fight and take all three back in court. News spread. People come from all quarters.

Everybody wonder what will Magistrate Batkin do to Bobby. Hepp and her daughter tell the magistrate what happen. Bobby had nothing to say. There was not a vacant space in the courtroom.

I want to hear what was going on for myself. Magistrate Batkin say that he believe that someone of the massas set up Bobby to attack Hepp, but he would have more sympathy for Bobby if Bobby did attack him instead. In addition to the serious contempt committed, I Robert Batkin, take objection to any man hitting a woman first. He tell the court, woman is the Creator's best gift to man and man must care and protect that gift. My boss R.S.D.

Goodwin see that he was going to deal heavy with Bobby and begin to beg for him. But Batkin give no ear to him. He sentence Bobby to six months hard labour along with twelve strokes, with the cat-o-nine. Massa George Goodwin ride behind the two horse guard that take Bobby to prison.

Planters were in uproar against Magistrate Batkin, but he did not notice them one bit. Some claim that Batkin did not care what he do because he has a dislike for the English massas.

Some time later, Bobby tell people that he get no cat-o-nine and only two weeks he stay in jail. He also say he have friends in high places, and that a friend in court is better than money in pocket. This old man call Batkin the record breaker, he was a man of my own heart. I agree with him when he said that woman is the Creator's best gift to man. The only man I know in my whole life that had such great regard for women in Antigua.

The Dye Wood tree also known as log wood tree. The wood produces a dye. The boat that transported the wood was also called the dye wood boat.

The old court house at Burke's Estate where Magistrate Batkin presided over many cases.

Batkin Tower, built during slavery, this historical monument still stands on Batkin's estate. The estate is situated in the south east of Antigua.

Parson Christopher of Lebanon maravian church of Sea View Farm (1863-1950). He helped his people to find work, kept them out of jail, and helped the sick. Rembered expecially for his great sermon at the turn of the twentieth century. The people of Sea View Farm proclaimed that no sermon could be better.

Empty carts being pulled by a steam locomotive. The locomotive became the most popular means of transportating sugar cane from the field to the factory

The Bagoon cart: unlike the open cart above was specifically made to prevent the sugar cane from falling out during transport. On arrival at the sugar factory, the side of the bagoon is opened by a lever and the cane falls out into what is called the "carrier". This is the beginning phase of the assemply line to process sugar cane into sugar.

195

May 13th, 1904 photo of the Antigua Sugar factory under construction

14
PAPA SAMMY THE METEOROLOGIST:
Points the way forward

Food is man's first request. Knowing this we have to depend on water, good soil, food plants, fish, animals and good planning. The bakkra always try hard to make sure these things are in place. Most of the time except if the going is real bad they will get what they set out to do. As I see it, the planters reign over this land will soon end completely. If we are to thrive after our people are at the control, this generation will have to begin to be trained in all aspects of development of the land.

To me, not many people are trying to obtain some of the knowledge that some of the planters have. The leaders of the land say so much bad bout all the bakkra that they are afraid now to tell people of any good work that any of them do. It is wrong to just throw them aside. When me talk the truth about the Goodwins or any other bakkra, nearly all the young people that hear me always say that me too love the old massas. That is the whole truth. This man don't hate a soul. Our land and sea contain the goods to support life. We own the waters, land, birds and animals too. We need the knowledge to harness these things properly.

One of the knowledgeable bakkra I have a good likeness for and one that the Union leaders should begin to use to educate the people is Franky Warneford, the Superintendent of Agriculture of this land, for many a year. A person must know plenty, plenty to be Superintendent of Agriculture. This was so all down the years. When I say plenty, I mean a whole tun about the agriculture business. Not just about sugar cane, but about the soil, the drainage of the land the weather-what is best to plant, where and when. The position was one of the most respected in the land. A great deal was always on the shoulders of the Superintendent of Agriculture since way back when, and up to this time. I think it will continue as long as man inhabit this land, unless we are going to get other countries to feed us. That is a heavy load.

The planters use to take any kind of bakkra and make them overseer. Family ties use to make some of them greatly respected managers. Any duncy head bakkra use to hold top positions and boast with it. But to be the Superintendent of Agriculture that bakkra have to come from good school, pass high, and know what he is about. I never know of a woman overseer or boss or manager, in this land. The bakkra misses never work, so when I talk of the bakkra is man a talking about.

Along time ago, I know a bakkra by the name of E.P. Turner. He was, at one time, the Superintendent of Agriculture. The Planters use to say "E.P. good, good". E.P. knows the stuff they would claim. Franky Warneford took over from him and there was a close association between the Goodwins and Franky as they use to call him. I am not at liberty to say how high Franky reach in school. All I know about his education is that the Goodwins say he went to McGrill University some where up in Canada. Franky Warneford improved drastically the Agriculture Station at Friars Hill and Bendals. According to what was said by Chief planter Alexander Moody Stuart at the Sugar Technologists Conference in 1949, in Antigua, the Friars Hill Agriculture Station was third in line in the

British West Indies. Ahead only by Jamaica and Trinidad. The British Government did not supply the money to keep three permanent specialists on the staff. According to Franky, the mother country think that an agricultural station of the standard of the one at Friars Hill was quite in order for the colony of Antigua. It did not need any further upgrading with additional specialists. The planters was not in agreement with the Mother Country. Agriculture was the life line and they always want the Mother Country to help them as much as possible in that field.

I always hear the planters say that the land has seven different soil type and five out of the lot are found at Friars Hill Agricultural Station. The planters use to rely heavily on the Friars Hill Station for guidance in almost everything. They carry out experiment after experiment on the various varieties of sugarcane and the soil more than anything else. The Station advise on what variety of sugar cane to plant and where. You would not even believe that the planters use to have details on every sugar cane field in the land. If North Sound Estate have forty fields of sugar cane, the North Sound planters would know what kind of cane or food to plant in each of them to get the best yield. Sugar cane fields carry a number to identify them. The soil type was registered in a book both at the estates and at Friars Hill.

The Superintendent of Agriculture know the kind of breed of cattle to bring to the land. The kind that can stand up to the hot sun and the dry weather. The best for haulage and ploughing and those for the production of meat and milk. That was the same thing for all the other animals and plants. Friars Hill was never without a Vet. It also had an animal hospital and a dairy farm. Milk was a precious thing in those days. Friars Hill produce large quantity of it. The Station use to supply the Hospital, the Poor House, the Leper Home and other government places along with some private bakkra, mostly those that do business in the city. Milk was on swing during my days.

The Friars Hill Station use to supply all kinds of animals to the people every year. They would roll drum and put them on sale. Only the chosen will get the best to buy. At one time, the planters use to breed and cross breed all kinds of animals at Friars Hill. I was always interested in the production of the mule. The station always have a big, big man donkey that they call the jack. This jack would be just about the average size of a horse. To get the production of the mule, the jack must jump[1] the horse and the picknee[2] that come from that horse is a mule. The mule is a trang , trang animal but cannot have a picknee. Back then, when a woman could not bring picknee people use to refer to her as a mule. At Friars Hill there was also a turkey farm. They sell them by the pair. Almost all the estates had a good amount of turkey. Don't talk bout the peacocks and peahens they were just beautiful to watch! At Friars Hill, there was also a whole flock of guiney bird and ducks.

Another thing, Friars Hill was hardly out of water. The weather would have to be very bad for that to happen. Five large ponds supply water. The ponds were well protected and all available channel lead to them to get maximum result from the rain. They use home made watering pans to water the plants. Adding top soil, applying the right manure and a system of periodic rest of certain areas prevent the soil at Friars Hill from being overwork. That make vegetables, the provisions and other plants grow to bang dog.[3]

Friars Hill use to have the bakkra that specialize in the grafting of trees. So too, it had the specialist on flowers. There was not a great house without a beautiful flower garden. The Sea View Farm flower pot makers use to rely on Friars Hill for regular business.

The Superintendent of Agriculture direct when to plant, and when to pluck up. The station was also able to tell from its record the many kinds of birds in the land. Friars Hill would have the record on the drainage of the whole land. That part which drains

[1] Mate with.

[2] Off spring.

[3] Grow abundantly.

good and that which does not. The area that is more salty than others and where water is located under the earth. The amount of rain that fall in the year and the area that get the least rain as well as the most. If there was another bakkra that use to do more work than the Superintendent of Agriculture, I would like someone to send me to that man. Every now and then, theAgriculture Superintendent use to have talks with various groups of planters on different estates and at Friars Hill concerning something about the agricultural business. It was always serious talking. I am always thankful for the many times when I get the rear privilege to stick round the group and hear a little of the talk.

I was never invited with the group, so don't misunderstand me. In a sense, nobody know me. I was only there because I have to take the bakkra and I would stay at the door or the window and cock me ear. At times, it was one member of the Goodwin family and at other times it could be all that go to the talk. The thing was, I hang around and no one drive me away. That was the privilege. I use to listen and take in what I can. After all, I use to plant the same sugar cane and the same food at me ground at Mossett and Osbourne. When the talk time happen to come round, it was good time for me. I always like to be around people who know what they are about. Sometimes when I hear Franky Warneford talking and explaining certain things to them bakkra, I get the feeling that I don't know a ting, not a Jesus ting.

One day, Franky Warneford ketch me writing down some of the things he was telling the group. After the talk was over, he take the paper from me. In a flash, I get frighten. A-wanda what was going to happen to me! I think that he was going to tell me to keep far away from the place. But I got a big relief when he hand me back the paper and tell me the only thing wrong was that I spell some words bad. I did not believe me ears when he tell me to come to hear him whenever I have the time even if my boss was not coming to the talk. Then he take back the paper from me and show it to my boss. Who tell him to do such a thing? My boss then get the understanding that I can write down the right thing and that bring him lazy. He did not want to spare the time to write anymore. Now and again, he would order me to take down everything for him. Sometimes he would not even go to hear for himself. I have to write down what Franky say and take them back to him. That was double work for me; I have to write the whole thing over to keep my own paper. But I learn a big lesson because of that. I find out that when I have to write the whole thing over, it stick firmly in me head. And sometimes I have to write the paper more than two-three times to make sure that anyone could understand me writing before I deliver it up. At most talks, the weather was the top ten.

The people before me and those of my time, always have keen interest in the weather. Few would have more interest in anything else. The kind of interest my mother use to have in the weather, make me use to say no man can match she - It would take plenty to pass her. My mother use to keep the rainfall record since she was a young gal. They date back to 1870. And believe me, two of a kind will always meet! And she meet she match. The woman, Louise Peters that I take and make wife, did have a much keener interest in the weather than me or my mother or any other person I know. She use to understand the rain gauge more than anybody I know. Anything my wife plant use to grow like token. My mother told us that it was a Methodist parson, one Reverand Roberts that teach her how to understand the rain gauge. My wife, on the other hand, say that it was her mother that she get the knowledge from.

My wife use to be so taken up with the weather that she use to chalk the board next to her bed any time rain fall. She had a funny disease. She would get sick with pain all over her body when rain set up. The pain would all vanish when the rain start to fall. She would mark from the biggest down pour to the slightest drizzle. She also put down even when the devil and wife a fight fu ham-bone[4]. Then, on old years day, she would count the chalk, write up the number of days on which rain fall for the year and compare it with last year.

4. There was a saying that when the rain is falling and sun is shining,
   that the devil and his wife fighting for hambone.

She would clean off the board and ready to start the new chalking from the first day of the year. She usually say that she practice from her mother who use to chalk the board for one Massa Willock of Bolans Estate. My wife religiously chalk the board and keep the number of days that rain fall on between 1910 and 1960. I have to give her all the rain records that I have each year. I continue to chalk the board up to one year after her death. I could not continue to knock-up with that any further. I couldn't tell you how she really manage to keep track of the rainfall every day for so long, maybe its because of her sickness - I only find the chalk from 1920 to 1960, the first ten years are lost.

From time to time when the weather happens to get hard, the saying would be, "more rain use to come in days of old than now." Franky tell the planters, at one of his talks at Diamond Estate, that the saying was just a belief and a belief can be very much out of order. Franky get none of the estate managers on his side. Norris Abbott, the Maginleys, the Goodwins, Walter Cooke, Leo Boyce, and poor me and all the rest was against him. While we were on our bible oath that less rain was bound to be coming at the present time than in previous years, so too, he was on his bible oath that there has not been any big change in the weather pattern for over sixty years. But he also say that continuing deforestation and lack of ground water could lead to less rain falling in the furure. It was a raging argument. Franky ask that everybody bring what record they have to get the argument trash out. Every man walk with them record to the next talk. My wife, the record keeper, just put them in me hand when I tell her the story. I carry them. Not a man expect me to have a record of the weather. That was for the bakkra. The big thing was, mine was for over a much longer period than for all of them. The planters could not believe it. What make it worse, I have the number of days that rain actually fall on, for many years. Suppose you hear how they praise me. I let them know the praise belong to me wife but they did not take me on.

Norris Abbott, Walter Cooke and Leo Boyce spend all morning checking the many records. At the end of it, they declare that Franky is the winner. Franky hold on to my record for some weeks. When he return them, he say to me, "I have to keep close to you. If I did know you in your young days, you surely would be a government man. You are a meteorologist." I did not know the word from Adam but he keep calling me the meteorologist and eventually I learn to call the word. He never stop telling me, "hide those records away in safe keeping," and he would go on to say, "one day they will prove to be very useful as they are right now." He then make it clear to me that I must not give my records to anybody. If I allow it, I will surely loose them. From that, me and he exchange the records of the rainfall of the land.

I also exchange them with Walter Cooke, manager of Burks Estate and Norris Abbott, manager of Diamond Estate. All three of us, put the rainfall records of the 1970's to 1980's, of the surrounding estates together. That fall between Diamond in the North to Burks in the mid-South East. At the end of 1980, I couldn't travel as I like. I could not go to see Cooke for us to check the rainfall anymore. Myself and Cooke use to have harty laugh, real harty laugh when the radio announcer make people hear day after day that only Coolidge rainfall they can talk bout - Cooke use to keep saying Soon they may never say anything at all bout the rain fall. These people don't even have the sense to mention Diamond and other places.

I think that enough rain come that can provide all the water needs of the land. Our people would have to devise ways and means of holding the water. As I talk, I get the gut feeling that the problem will get worse. There is no longer any deliberate guiding of the water to dams and ponds and ghuts. Most of them now level with the surface. The land is like a house without spouting. The water is left to find its own way when the good Lord send the showers. Heavy down pour now wash out the land and cause it to dry out quicker.

The grass that spring up so readily after the showers do not remain green for long. Now is the time to begin to build new dams, clear out the guts and build more ponds. The planting of trees is a must, I have not seen this happen for many a year. In fact the new people pluck them up and never replant them.

Anybody that have anything to do with this land, know from morning that there is a water problem. Long drought ever so often. The big, big thing is the water problem. No point keep on crying. Tackle the problem! Now is the time to start to build large dams all over the land. Build them with more length than width so that trees can protect the water from the broiling sun for part of the day.

From my knowledge the greater portion of the land drain in a north and northwesterly direction washing out to the sea. The new know how in the world of today will make it easier to build the dams or anything for that matter.

Build at least one water catchment in every village. Large village like All Saints and Liberta should have more than one. Four would do. No small catchment. Cement cheap. Useless building a catchment less than two hundred feet in length and fifty feet in depth. Put the village council squarely in charge of the catchment and anything to do with water. Tax every villager to help pay for the catchment. Who can't give some days of free labour or donate material would have to pay from their pocket. Put aside some of the sugar cess money to help people build cistern. Start with the new houses. Everyone should have a cistern, never mind the size of the house. After a time, the size will improve. The cistern would already be in place.

Me talk to Donald Sheppard, my Council Representative, and he agree with me. Maybe he can't convince the rest. My argument must have sound foolish, hard and impossible because not a movement I see year after year. If the people think small, then my argument will surely fail. Just marshall up the people. Bet you life the fruit will come! And come quick at least within forty years. One good dam in every ten years from now would produce at least three

before the century close. Forty years sound long but don't do anything and you will see how quick the years roll on. Do stubbon
now! The next generation would be better off. The new know how
is turning sea water into fresh water. That is a good back up. That
can't keep the land moist nor keep the water table high enough for
the farming needs of the people. Water beget water. A sensible
damming programme would help to do just that. It will make us
feed ourself and provide goods for other necessities of life. "If the
leaders use the new know-how of the sea fully it would add plenty
more on the table The argument in the land now is Statehood, in
charge of you self. If a man can't feed himself he can't properly be
in charge of himself. If we do not do something to help some one
when we can, if we do not work hard to lay a good foundation for
the coming generation, our tenure in this life would be useless. And
I believe, that would be the worst thing to happen to any of God's
children."

The last time I go to talk with Franky was sometime in the
early 1960's. This time at Betty's Hope. He tell me that Friars Hill
Agricultural Station will be no more. The Government decide to
close it in order to give way to a new oil refinery. Nothing else was
talk about but the end of Friars Hill Argricultural Station. It was a
sad meeting. Franky and the others decide to put a letter together
to send to Administrator Turbutt asking him to choose another
place. Some of the places I think about was- at the edge of
Johnston's Point and Darkwood in the south of the island. At the
southwest end of Liberta was another and Crabbs Peninsula and
also south of Dunbars. But useless anybody argue, nobody listen.
All I know is that the generation to come will pay dearly for that
decision. The decision seem to scatter the planters. I don't remember going to another talk after that. I can tell anybody that I also
mourn because I did not hear Franky talking on pest control, food
production, the carrying out of experiment and the result of those
experiments[5]. I soon go bout my business[6] - so take care of these
records[7].

The farmer will remain king in any age. The destroying of Friars Hill Agricultural Station compel me to believe that the new breed of people, in this land, don't think too much of the future. But to me, it's still not too late to start.

5. The closure of the Friars Hill Agriculture Station brought an end to proper record keeping on Agriculture, pest control, food production, experiments, the rainfall and other vital environmental issues. It also brought about the destruction of previous records. Persistent research is unable to provide to date, any records of the rainfall of Antigua and Barbuda before 1960. And those after 1960 refer to the Coolidge area only. Papa Sammy's record from the late 1800 encompassing the whole island is perhaps the only one that can be found for future reference.

6. I soon die.

7. We suspect that the documenting of rainfall in the various regions of Antigua and Barbuda kept by Papa Sammy before 1960 is the only record that can be refered to in the future.

Papa Sammy

Norris Abbott

Franklyn Warneford

Walter Cook

Part of the so called "meterological team" who used to exchange records and discuss Antigua rainfall between 1910 and 1980.

Brief Weather History as Recorded by Papa Sammy
Number of days on which rain fell between 1920-1962
Across Freemans Village, Sanderson, Mossette, Osbourne Pasture,
Duers and Collins.

Year	Days	Year	Days
1920	192	1942	132
1921	181	1943	128
1922	166	1944	130
1923	177	1945	120
1924	173	1946	147
1925	164	1947	190
1926	168	1948	175
1927	179	1949	149
1928	190	1950	167
1929	198	1951	153
1930	195	1952	192
1931	160	1953	188
1932	169	1954	171
1933	159	1955	183
1934	174	1956	160
1935	166	1957	197
1936	164	1958	181
1937	190	1959	182
1938	171	1960	163
1939	171	1961	172
1940	180	1962	181
1941	150		

The Average Monthly Distribution of rainfall from 1870-1962

	Massette	Osbourne	Duers	Collins
January	2.50	2.36	2.60	2.55
February	1.70	1.65	1.25	1.58
March	1.40	1.45	1.44	1.43
April	2.30	2.24	2.20	2.05
May	3.50	3.26	4.28	4.36
June	3.42	2.95	3.10	3.00
July	3.00	3.25	3.64	3.50
August	4.20	4.35	4.00	3.98
September	5.00	4.50	4.80	4.58
October	4.20	4.00	5.00	4.60
November	5.00	4.92	4.90	5.30
December	3.00	2.90	3.00	2.98

Antigua Annual Rainfall In Inches from the year 1870-1980					
Year	Rainfall (in.)	Year	Rainfall (in.)	Year	Rainfall (in.)
1870	39.00	1906	54.16	1945	40.90
1871	52.00	1907	44.50	1946	36.12
1872	42.20	1908	44.00	1947	2910
1873	37.30	1909	46.12	1948	36.41
1874	30.06	1910	32.17	1949	49.03
1875	28.78	1911	35.26	1950	48.07
1876	42.20	1912	31.16	1951	60.30
1877	50.10	1913	44.20	1952	55.00
1878	47.19	1914	35.80	1953	28.29
1879	63.50	1915	57.30	1954	39.00
1880	49.68	1918	37.87	1955	43.15
1881	54.12	1919	50.50	1956	43.15
1882	33.04	1920	30.09	1957	43.37
1883	55.51	1921	30.32	1958	46.00
1884	44.90	1922	34.35	1959	37.97
1885	44.50	1923	32.12	1960	36.20
1886	47.78	1924	42.20	1961	38.40
1887	43.68	1925	31.17	1962	50.20
1888	44.23	1926	52.30	1963	46.18
1889	76.00	1927	48.17	1964	34.00
1890	33.00	1928	32.00	1965	38.40
1891	50.01	1930	25.51	1966	26.90
1892	39.40	1931	48.62	1967	31.50
1893	39.20	1932	59.40	1968	29.10
1894	39.50	1933	42.12	1969	51.00
1895	53.12	1934	43.00	1970	66.20
1896	64.00	1935	38.31	1971	43.30
1897	39.67	1936	63.20	1972	40.25
1898	48.85	1937	47.28	1973	24.90
1899	46.89	1938	44.75	1974	54.00
1900	36.95	1939	30.00	1975	38.00
1901	60.00	1940	37.37	1976	37.30
1902	60.31	1941	49.37	1977	39.50
1903	4450	1942	50.26	1978	53.00
1904	38.12	1943	49.08	1979	70.50
1905	30.20	1944	37.13	1980	33.50

Monthly Distribution of Rainfall (Antigua Station)

	Whole Island Graynors 1985-1962	Yeptons 1905–1962	Gunthropes 1899-1962	High Point 1900-1962	Mount Pelier 1912-1962	Cassada Gardens 1914-1962	Hodges Bay 1901-1962	Bendals 1917-1962	New Division 1911-1962	Diamond 1905-1962
January	2.68	2.24	3.21	2.05	2.53	2.64	2.56	3.45	3.08	2.26
February	1.60	1.52	1.80	1.49	1.50	1.48	1.23	1.98	1.83	1.65
March	1.71	1.48	1.92	1.32	1.58	1.43	1.37	2.05	1.90	1.65
April	2.24	2.27	2.59	2.08	2.51	2.05	1.94	2.51	2.20	1.51
May	3.44	3.63	3.73	2.97	3.24	3.62	4.14	4.07	3.37	3.26
June	3.24	3.38	3.53	2.77	3.00	3.12	3.01	4.12	2.77	3.27
July	3.63	3.31	3.83	2.89	3.02	3.01	2.92	4.32	4.22	3.26
August	4.62	4.65	5.10	3.77	4.08	4.93	4.79	5.78	5.65	4.14
September	5.38	5.26	5.20	3.79	4.95	4.99	5.22	6.95	3.79	4.80
October	5.13	4.89	6.01	4.86	4.47	4.71	4.87	6.36	5.71	4.50
November	5.68	5.20	5.93	5.16	4.79	4.73	4.02	6.84	5.99	5.13
December	3.49	3.23	3.63	2.82	3.38	3.43	3.43	3.71	3.75	3.20

1. Index of Places

Green Castle 18
English People 19
Rat Island: is a little hill 19, 157
Fort James, Fryes and Hyde Estates 20
Fig Tree Hill 24, 75, 76, 77
Christian Valley 28
Map pleasure ride 30
Collins and Duers Estate 35
Yag 42
Nigeria – Montserrat 42
Hawksbill 43, 79, 80
Stony Hill 43
Old Road, Parham, Ottos, Grays Farm and Woods 48
Sick Hark, Shekerly Hills 52, 61
Mussette Spring, Massa Ruin, Essess Hole 61
Tom More Spring 62
Anglican Cathedral Yard 63
Bridge - A - Peace 77
Irish Hengman Stone 79
Leper Colony 157
Barbuda, Cockrum Pond Burial Ground 162
Lebanon Moravian Church 163
Nedds Bay, Gaud Point, Galley Bay, Deep Bay Point, Goat Hill 80
Crepplegate Bay, Salt Pond, Union Bay, Week Point 80
Lablaliah Bay, Hawksbill Rock, Pelican Rock, St Georges Bay 80
St Georges Estate, Cold Point, Pinchin Bay, Pearns Point 80
Five Islands, Five Islands Estate 80
Ma Dudie , Dada Pinny 87 – 89
Freemans Village 132
Nelsons Dockyard 89 – 92
Lady B 89
Vernons Estate 94
Warner Estate 99, 128
Gilbert Sunday School, Sunday School Golden Text 103
Graynors Estate 110

Willikies, Cedar Grove, Crabb Hill and Johnsons Point 113
Cades Bay, Merica, All Saints Village 119 – 120
Old Road 127, 129, 131, 133 - 134, 136, 139 – 140
Winthorpe 137
Parish of St. Phillips, Betty's Hope 145
Willikies 152
Long Lane Estate 169
Frias Hill, Skerritts and Bendals 167
Barnacle Point 169
Mount Pleasant, Martinique 177
Jail 179
Mingo, Nyampas, Nyampas Pond 180, 181
Potter, Sanderson 182
Dominica, Antigua 183
Winthorpe 184
McGill University, Sugar Technologists Conference 199
Friars Hill, Jamaica, Trinidad, North Sound 199
Animal Hospital and Dairy Farm 200
Diamond Estate 203, 204
Friars Hill Agriculture Station 206
Johnsons Point, Darkwood 206
Crabbs Penninsular, Dunbars 206
Public Works 172
Freeman's Village Methodist Church 173
Duers, U-Mans Estate and Jail 173
Falmouth 174
English Harbour, Piccadily Dance House, Zandy Shop 175
Mobile Prison 176
Empire, Merica, St Thomas 177
Elizabeth, Susana, Grey Hound Galley 119
Jarpots 130
Bellman Tree 132
Duck Weed, Donkey Milk 137

2.   Index of Events

In 1847 Gregory of Briggins pray for hurricane to come and blow away
the trash houses 67
Hurricane 1848   67
21 people could not be found   69
Name of Free Villages and how they were named   72 – 75
Play Fight   76
Slave Revolt, Gallows, French took Antigua in the 1660's 79
Fire 18" Century   79
House of Assembly 1649   81
Young gal disappear   86
Speechless and in disbelief   89
Ringing the bell at the base   90
Barking over a nine day period   91
They would torture and kill them, captivity 92
Slave from Warner beaten to death in 1830   99
Moravians and Methodist doing all they could   100
Public School Start in the 1850's   100
Moravians find out that when exslaves go to buy goods slave masters
were robbing them blind 101, 112
Teaching how to count money   101
Anglicans tell them teaching was out of place   102
Between 1863 and 1864 a good number of population
loose them life   147
Poison, Fire main weapon 147
Up to 1866 villages were still going up   148
Priests and Parsons say no riot   148
The generation of 1860's   149
The Darius Phrase, Debble Malone   150
Freemans Village down to 3 houses   151
By 1870 all the main villages around Vernons and Parham
were gone 151
1871 Hurricane, Plantation life start full force again   151
Beginning of 1870's all but three vanish   151
Real filthy land between the 1870's up to well into the 1900's   153
New Years Sunday 1890   157

Midwives 1890   158
Governor Haynes Smith ask that the men chimb up   159 – 167
Lawyers and Officers   160
In the 1880's Rats descended on the land like a plague   165
Mongoose turn to Massa children, Mongoose traps   166
Nega Man allowed to own dogs   166
Norman Inquiry   167
Gunthorpes Sugar Factory   167
1714, Dupunt and Bride fell into the gulley   24
Fig Tree and Uooge Hill Roads become safer at the end of
the 1720's   26
Go on the Pleasure Ride in 1899   27 – 28
Map, Nugent Time   40 – 45
William Joseph landed at Parham 1638   42
Chief of Police Lovell   45
Made fish pots out of chink wood   46
Counting walking steps   49
Tar Rope, mahoe bark   50
Two kinds of rub   52
Barking of the body   53
Head Tie and Belly Band   54
Wheel barrows imported late 1830's – 1840's   56
Holding of Singing Meeting and Tea Meeting   57 – 58
First Sunday in August   58
Muddy Wash   62
New Freedom 1834, Earthquake 1843   65
Massa Jackson of Belmot put to the Assembly to
bring in East Indians   66
Assembly pass law to bring in Portuguese   66
40 Villages put up near the end of 1840   67
Hawksbill haunch   93
Giving left over food   95
Constant war between the new village people and the planters   96
Smoking and drinking   97
Humming and singing   98
Slapping slaves in the face   98
Swinging away her Ma, Pem – Pem – Pem   99

Between the 1707's and 1750's Antigua reach the peak
with the number of sugar estates 143
At the time of the freedom   65 – 77
Wheel Wright, the carpenter, cooper and blacksmith start
to act up   144
The Goodwin Record Book stated the family had 248 slaves
between 1835 and 1850 145 Goodwin slaves dwindled to 50 145
17,000 people live across the land in 1863 – 64, only five
and one half thousand were male 145
Beauty Box, Deep Sorrow   108
Put me up and put me down   109
Moravian start concert in 1850   109
Making clothes   111
The dolly 112
English was not the mother tongue   112
Anglican School Room in the 1930's   118
Anglican Bishop, Garvey 118
The Nugent Family in Jamaica and Antigua   118
Garvey talk well and proper   120
Queen Conch Shell   120
Neptune set folks on him   186
Benna on the whole jail term   186
Crowd run over into the street   187
Picking time   189
Get no cat – o – nine   192
Rainfall records   202
She use to chalk the board   203
Continuing deforestation and lack of ground water   203
Seven standard exam start after 1914   171
School use to hold plenty concerts 172
Blazing of his back   172
Nelly Robinson night school   173
Manners them, Mack prison gang   174
Jail man feast   175
1939 World War   177
Dye Wood boat   180
Donkey lick off Nyampas hand   181

Bakkra pass law to beat anyone found working obeah 182
Sammy ask coffee woman Neptune to driff every body
from around Blair 185
Between 1900 and 1906 four Governors went through
Government House 167
1902 planters put up new building near Government House 168
Inspector of Schools came to the land in 1912 170

3.   Index of People and Groups

Greedy Ruin 22
Clive Dupunt 24 – 25
Governor Matthew 25
Hamilton 25
Admiral Lord Nelson 28
Sunday School 34
Massa MaGregor, letter to Secretary of State 36, 48, 51
Anglican Church people wage bitter war against apprenticeship 36
Number of slaves in 1929 – 2900 37
Speaker of the Assemble, Dr. Nicholas Nugent loose the vote
on period of apprenticeship 37
S.A. Hill founder of Hills Secondary School 39
R. S. D. Goodwin 17
All Saints Anglican Church 38
Maurice Michael, Donald Sheppard 39
Jumbia. 41 – 47, 57, 59, 60, 78, 82, 86, 88, 92, 96 – 147, 150
Massa William Joseph, Old Goat 42
The Kings land, Names of people that put up villages 43 - 44
Methodist 44 – 110
Moravian .47 – 51, 56 – 110
Fisher woman 46
Motherless gals 55
Massa Redwood, Osbourne, William Gregory, Dunbars 56
Church Slaves 57
Exslaves get food and gave out prizes 58

Antigua Weekly Tines 70
Free Press, Scotland 71
William Billinghurst, John Billinghurst. 78 – 89, 90 – 91
Radison and family, George and Affie Goodwin 82
Countess Sebastian, Mandy Hector, Millers great house 82
Hawksbill comb 83
Pantoon 84
Fun house – leap house .84 – 86
New Day 84
Leap Day 85
Colonel Monk, Monks Hill 92
Soldiers and planters 92
Trash huts 92
Best looking people, most big foot people, most red mouth people 154
Cibonies, Caribs, Arawaks 18
Vickey, Bill Bertie 140
Frank Willikie, Massa Bolans 152
The filthiest estate 154
Population run down between the 1860's and 1880's 155
Population pick up in the 1890's 155
Governor Haynes Smith 155 – 156, 160 – 161, 163 – 164
Board of Health Workers 156
Church of England 158
Guss Henry of Woods Estate 159
Mother's touch, Court House 160
Lady Bethel, Massa Doughall, John Tudway, Mark Tudway 161
Massa Hinds 162
Parson Christopher, Governor F and F 163
Nellie Robinson 163, 170
Anglican Bishop 170
George Moody-Stuart, Massa Edwards 168
Sour Betty, Parsons Mauls jail, prisoners 168
Leeward Islands Jail, Big Court, Jail House 268
Antonio Camacho, The Camacho Family 169
Jack Lard, Joe Knight, Mark Barretto 169
Briggins, Mount Pleasant, Stoney Hill 169
Bastard in Secondary School 170

Giant Corn Mill Drivers, Animal Doctor 146
Animal Doctor, Mother Country, Colour Red 146
Nellie Robinson 171
Nellie Robinson High School 172
Joe Blake, "We de whites", Charlie Cockram 172
Alfred Mack 173
Neville, Bucksie, Tranie 174
Draggy, Massa Noble 175
Massa Noble, The Governor 176
Sydney Christian, Lady Nelson 177
Local Constable, Magistrate 179
Magistrates, Constable, Massa Affie Goodwin 180
Robert Batkin, Missy Crighton 180
Horse guard, Dab Dab 181
Dab Dab, Magistrate Batkin, Constable Roy Man 182
Massa Noel, Cyril Bago, Miss Crighton 182
Professor Daniel, The Menzes Family 183
Menzes Family, Magistrate Dyett, Sammy Martin 184
Blair, Neptune, Sammy 184
Madam Neptune 185
Sammy, Freddy Dubang, Manny Emanuel 186
Marty Hope, Magistrate Dyette, Batkin 186
Dubang's Mother, Marty Hope, Mama Silly 187
Clarry, Goerge Bournes, Constable Martin, Magistrate Batkin 187
Mama Sily, Magistrate 188, 189
Batkin 188, 189, 191
Coffee Woman Pelle, Coffee Woman Maggie, Jacob. 188, 189, 190
Claxton 'a bossom friend of Jacobs' 189
Old Elizabeth, Mason, Hepp 190, 191
Bobby Williams, Massa George Goodwin 191, 192
E. P Turner 198
Moody-Stuart 199
Mosette & Osbourne 201
Frankie Waneford 202
Reverend Roberts 202

Norris Abbott, The Maginleys, Goodwins, Walter Cooke,
Leo Boyce   203, 204
Village Council   205
Donald Sheppard   206
Administrator Turbutt   206

About the Author

SIR KEITHLYN SMITH

Senator Sir Keithlyn Smith of Antigua-Barbuda is one of the founding members of the Antigua and Barbuda Workers Union. He served two terms in the Upper House of Antigua and Barbuda and also held the position of Secretary-General of the Antigua-Barbuda Workers Union from 1970-2002. He has left an indelible mark in his pursuit for social, economical and political advancements for the people of Antigua and Barbuda. He is the author of *No Easy Push-over,* co-author of *To Shoot Hard Labour* and also published his work *Symbol of Courage.*